The Blessed Isle

Other Long Island Studies Institute (LISI) publications of related interest:

Long Island Studies Series (Heart of the Lakes Publishing)
Evoking a Sense of Place, 1988
Robert Moses: Single-Minded Genius, 1989
Long Island and Literature, 1989
The Aerospace Heritage of Long Island, 1989
Long Island: The Suburban Experience, 1990
Long Island Architecture, 1991
From Airship to Spaceship, 1991

Suburbia Re-examined (Greenwood Press), 1990
To Know the Place: Teaching Local History (LISI), 1986
Cumulative Index, Nassau County Historical Society Journal, 1958–1988 (LISI), 1989
The Calderone Theatres on Long Island: An Introductory Essay and Description of the Calderone Theatre Collection at Hofstra University (LISI), 1991

The Blessed Isle

Hal B. Fullerton
and His Image of Long Island
1897–1927

by
Charles L. Sachs

Heart of the Lakes Publishing
Interlaken, New York
1991

Unless otherwise stated, all images are by H. B. Fullerton and from the collection of the Suffolk County Historical Society, Riverhead, New York. The Historical Society's catalogue numbers are indicated in parentheses. Picture captions shown in *italics* denote titles for the images that were published or inscribed by the photographer.

Sachs, Charles L.
    The Blessed Isle : Hal B. Fullerton and his image of Long Island, 1897–1927 / by Charles L. Sachs.
    104 p.   cm.
    Includes bibliographical references and index.
    1. Long Island (N.Y.)—History.   2. Fullerton, Hal B., 1857–1935.   3. Long Island (N.Y.)—History—Pictorial works.   4. Long Island (N.Y.)—Biography.
I. Title.
F127.L8S26   1991
974.7′21—dc20   90–27112

ISBN: 1–55787–078–0

Manufactured in the United States of America

A *quality* publication of
Heart of the Lakes Publishing
Interlaken, New York 14847

Contents

Loading Railroad Car with Farm Exhibits, Medford, 1912. Edith Fullerton is at the wheel of the automobile (149.7.747).

Foreword

Hal B. Fullerton became a Special Agent for the Long Island Railroad in 1897, and devoted his life thereafter to promoting Long Island, which he called the "Blessed Isle." A serious—and quite talented—amateur photographer, he used his camera in his publicity efforts for the railroad. For three decades he promoted Long Island: bicycling and good roads, as well as the railroad; recreation and tourism; country life in estates and suburban homes; and horticulture and agriculture. As director of the Railroad's Agriculture Department, he conducted experimental farms at Wading River and Medford from 1905 through the 1920s, to demonstrate the productivity of the soil in the "waste lands" of the scrub oak and pine barrens.

The turn of the century was an important transition period in Long Island's history. Brooklyn and the western towns of geographic Long Island joined politically with New York City. Suffolk and newly created Nassau County were increasingly less dependent on water transportation and maritime pursuits and redirecting their focus westward, linked by the railroad to the metropolis. The Long Island Railroad had built new branch lines and extended others. In the early 1900s, electrification and tunnels to Manhattan further improved access. It was an age of railroad suburbs, country homes, boarding house resorts, and market-farming agriculture. In these years Hal Fullerton promoted a vision of Long Island which emphasized its natural beauty and bounty, made accessible to city dwellers by the railroad.

Fullerton's romantic image of Long Island was of an earlier agrarian age, already in the process of change with unprecedented population growth and, by the 1920s, the growing popularity of the automobile. Though development slowed in the Great Depression, after World War II, farms and fields gave way to subdivision tract developments in automobile suburbs; shopping centers and industry proliferated, changing the landscape and built environment.

It is difficult to document the impact of Fullerton's efforts either in increasing the railroad's passenger and freight traffic or promoting Long Island agriculture. The railroad's demonstration farms and agricultural publications by the Fullertons were forerunners of government-sponsored extension services, and it is probably not a coincidence that the state created one of its first agricultural schools in Farmingdale. (It is now SUNY College of Technology at Farmingdale and no longer offers agricultural courses.) Yet Suffolk County remains today the leading agricultural county in the state in terms of the value of its products.

Hal Fullerton's most significant and enduring contribution is certainly his extensive photographic documentation of Long Island at the turn of the century and in the early decades of the twentieth century. The Suffolk County Historical Society received an extensive collection of Fullerton's glass plate negatives and other photographic materials in 1949 from Harry T. Tuthill, who at that time owned "Lorelope," the former Fullerton home in East Setauket. The Society's collection records indicate that the gift was made through Samuel B. Cross, a friend to the Society, who was well known as a local historian. Cross worked as Assistant Civil Engineer for the County Highway Department under Tuthill, who was then Superintendent of Highways in Suffolk. According to oral tradition, the collection was about to be discarded at the town landfill when it was saved by Mr. Cross, who arranged for the donation to the Suffolk County Historical Society.

The Society's Fullerton holdings, comprised of the Tuthill donation and images that have since been acquired, consists of 503 eleven-by-fourteen-inch glass negatives, 1,670 smaller glass negatives (mostly five-by-seven-inch, but including five-by-eight-inch and several other sizes), 185 lantern slides and glass display transparencies, 38 nitrate-based negatives, and 10 Lumiere autochromes.

The Society has displayed Fullerton prints in its exhibits, and some historians have utilized them, most notably Frederick Lightfoot, Linda Martin, and Bette Weidman, in *Suffolk County, Long Island in Early Photographs, 1867–1951* (Dover, 1984). Although Fullerton himself had been largely forgotten beyond the walls of the Historical Society's building, the collection had long been recognized as an important resource.

A major preservation effort began in 1987, when the Society received funding from the New York State Council on the Arts (NYSCA), the New York State Discretionary Grant Program for the Conservation/Preservation of Library Resource Materials, the Henry L. O'Brien Foundation, and the Daily News Foundation. The multi-phased project involved cataloguing, stabilizing, conserving, and assessing the Fullerton Collection. Further discussion of the scope of this work is beyond the limitations of this foreword; however, it should be noted that the conditions under which the collection was stored and the organization of the collection were dramatically improved through the guidance of Mr. Michael Hager, formerly the Negative Archivist at the International Museum of Photography in Rochester. Mr. Hager served as principal project consultant and, among other things, advised the Society's staff on state-of-the-art methods of reproducing the Fullerton images to a more stable format. Work on this phase continues, but progress depends on the availability of funds.

A 1988 exhibition planning grant from NYSCA provided the opportunity for a unique joint venture. Charles L. Sachs was invited to resume and bring to completion his earlier Fullerton research and to develop the results into an exhibit and accompanying catalogue. Additional support from NYSCA, the Henry L. O'Brien Foundation, the Charles Davis Estate, and Suffolk County (Patrick Halpin, Suffolk County Executive) enabled the final script editing and the installation of the exhibit.

"The Blessed Isle: Hal B. Fullerton and His Image of Long Island" opened at the Historical Society in Riverhead on June 23, 1990. As guest curator, Mr. Sachs researched and meticulously documented Fullerton's life and career. The exhibit was accomplished through the dedicated work of volunteers, staff, and consultants. The Society is particularly indebted to Hal and Edith Fullerton's daughters, Eleanor Ferguson and Hope Zarensky, who, along with their families, so willingly shared both their memories and their family collections to make the exhibition and this book possible.

Charles Sachs considers Fullerton's work as a railroad publicist in the context of other railroad promotional efforts of the era. Interwoven through the text are the contributions of Hal Fullerton's wife and partner, Edith Loring Fullerton. She played an important role, particularly in the agricultural work, and her life exemplifies the growing opportunities open to women in the twentieth century. Sachs also deals with a number of other themes important to broader historical topics, including photography, transportation, publicity and advertising, suburbanization, and the development of Long Island agriculture. Through a biographical focus, we have a perspective of the aesthetic vision of the photographer who created unparalleled visual images of turn-of-the-century Long Island.

This publication is a collaboration between the Suffolk County Historical Society in Riverhead and the Long Island Studies Institute at Hofstra University. Charles L. Sachs's research on Fullerton for the Historical Society resulted in a more extensive essay than could be incorporated in an exhibit catalog. Because this is a significant contribution to Long Island history, the Long Island Studies Institute of Hofstra University agreed to cooperate in publishing the book as part of its Long Island Studies series. The black and white photographs in the exhibition and this book were produced by Jonathan Penney. The Society is indebted to Harvey A. Weber for his advice and for the reproduction of the color images. Though only a sample of the rich treasure trove of photographs can be included in this volume, we are pleased to reproduce some of the rare hand-tinted display transparencies and autochrome plates for the first time. We trust this volume will make more people aware of these images—and the man who created them.

Wallace W. Broege, Director   Natalie A. Naylor, Director
Suffolk County Historical Society   Long Island Studies Institute

The connecting train from the first train through the East River tunnels arrives at Medford, LIRR Experimental Station No. 2, September 8, 1910 (detail from 149.7.647). The opening of a direct rail route across Long Island to the new Pennsylvania Station was widely celebrated throughout the New York area, heralding a major expansion in commuter service.

Preface

Anyone who is interested in exploring the visual landscape or iconography of Long Island's past will find the photographs of Hal B. Fullerton (1857–1935) and the Suffolk County Historical Society's collection of his negatives immensely valuable. Fullerton's work was so extensive, inclusive, and pervasive that it is difficult to imagine the Island's appearance at the turn of the twentieth century without subconsciously conjuring up his pictures.

Although I did not realize the significance at the time, I first came across Fullerton's image-making during 1977–78, while I was working as a graduate intern in the Library and Archives of The Museums at Stony Brook, organizing and evaluating their collection of historic photographs. In the course of researching the collection and preparing an exhibit and catalogue, *A Casual Witness: Photographs from the Hawkins Family Collection* (1978), I began to gather material on the history of photography on Long Island in the nineteenth and early twentieth centuries. This brought Fullerton's name, as well as several different editions of his *Unique Long Island* pamphlet series and two small, previously undocumented groups of vintage photographs, to my attention. It also led me to the Suffolk County Historical Society where, while gathering biographical data and seeing prints from the original negatives, I made the acquaintance of the extremely helpful staff. Through these contacts, I started the lengthy, drawn out, personal research effort that eventually culminated in the present volume.

To build on my completed work at Stony Brook, during odd moments of free time in 1978 and 1979, I visited museums, historical societies, and libraries throughout the Island, sampling images and collecting material on early local photographers. I originally planned to survey the entire field of historic photography on Long Island to develop a major book and exhibition on this subject. However, I soon found that an extraordinary wealth of information and imagery survived pertaining just to Fullerton—material clearly warranting more thorough examination and analysis—and I began to concentrate my research in this direction.

It was during this period that I first met and interviewed the photographer's younger daughter, Eleanor Ferguson, who was then living nearby in St. James. Mrs. Ferguson identified pictures I had brought, but more importantly shared her recollections and opinions, suggested other places and people to visit, and loaned me a copy of her superb written reminiscences (*As I Remember It*, 1978). She also allowed me to examine her collection of old family memorabilia, books, and papers, and particularly the vintage photographic prints and lantern slides by her father. As a result of this and subsequent visits, I began to amass a sizeable research file of unpublished material on Fullerton.

Unfortunately, work on this project proceeded more slowly than anticipated and was finally interrupted by more immediate personal and professional concerns. After a ten-year hiatus—and the encouragement of the Suffolk County Historical Society—I returned to my boxes of files and notes and reexamined Fullerton. During the intervening period, the Historical Society had succeeded in cataloguing, stabilizing, and conserving its Fullerton holdings. The next phase of work was to develop an exhibition to showcase the collection, and it was with this endeavor that Society Director Wallace W. Broege, aware of my earlier interest, sought my collaboration. The present volume, prepared as an adjunct of the exhibit, is a cooperative effort of the Suffolk County Historical Society and Hofstra University's Long Island Studies Institute.

Many people have contributed to this effort. At the Suffolk County Historical Society, I would like to thank Wallace W. Broege, director, and Marsha Hamilton, former curator, for initiating the exhibition project and for their continued assistance and support. Others at the Society deserve to be acknowledged as well, including curator Barbara E. Austen and consulting exhibit coordinator Susan Klaffky, for their work on the installation, administrative assistant Diane F. Perry, librarian Joanne Brooks, and curatorial assistant Elaine S. Timin. At Hofstra, I am most grateful to Natalie A. Naylor, director of the Long Island Studies Institute, who provided valuable comments and suggestions on the text and without whose interest this publication would not have been possible. Thanks also to Lisa MacLeman for her careful editing of the text.

Research for a work such as this naturally depends on the generosity of a great many individuals and institutions. To the photographer's daughters, Eleanor Ferguson and Hope Fullerton Tuttle Zarensky, I owe particular thanks. Both freely gave their knowledge, memories, and opinions. Mrs. Zarensky offered helpful leads and insight into her family's history, especially the early years of her parents' marriage, through correspondence, notes, and many written suggestions. Mrs. Ferguson provided extremely useful reminiscences and unlimited access to a virtual "treasure trove" of rare old family photographs, drawings, manuscripts, newsclippings, and other important documentary evidence, which proved indispensable. I am also indebted to her sustained belief in the project, her hospitality, and friendship over many years. Her daughters Anne F. Nauman and Edith House helped, as well, by reviewing drafts of the text and sharing additional historical data and family materials.

Others who contributed information, research sources, and access to collections include the following: Andrew Havrisko, St. James, NY; Ron Ziel, Water Mill, NY; Ken Finkel, Library Company of Philadelphia; Sarah McNear, Allentown Art Museum, Allentown, PA; Brooklyn Historical Society Library; Hofstra University, Long Island Studies Institute; Huntington Historical Society; The Museums at Stony Brook, Library/Archives; New York Public Library, Research Division; Port Jefferson Public Library; Queensborough Public Library, Long Island Division, Jamaica; and Society for the Preservation of Long Island Antiquities, Setauket, NY.

My greatest debt remains to Debby, Sarah, and Adam who inspired and sustained my repeated journeys through the Blessed Isle, helped me keep my balance, and made it all worthwhile.

Charles L. Sachs

Hal B. Fullerton, Huntington, c. 1910. Photographer unknown. Courtesy, Ferguson Collection.

Hal B. Fullerton and His Image of Long Island

Introduction

Discovering Long Island when he was about forty years of age, Hal B. Fullerton apparently became obsessed with it. The discovery came at a strategic moment in history, the decade of the 1890s, when the nation and New York metropolis were emerging from a harsh economic depression. By the end of the period, the political boundaries of Long Island were radically altered when the City of Brooklyn and a portion of what had been Queens County became part of New York City. In this decisive decade, Hal Fullerton, approaching middle age, was about to begin an exciting new life on Long Island.

Long Island served as Fullerton's personal catalyst, as both a source of inspiration and an outlet for his varied creative interests. Here was not simply a convenient, healthful place to reside, conduct business, or enjoy a holiday. Fullerton found or forged on Long Island an ideal landscape and a symbolic home. He called it the "Blessed Isle" and he advertised and promoted its virtues and value—its "advantages"—with an exuberance, tenacity, wit, and imagination perhaps only possible during that progressive era. He claimed Long Island to be "the most richly and beautifully Nature-endowed region of the whole United States, Canada, Mexico, and the West Indies."[1] Certainly, few before him had dedicated themselves so fervently to this cause, and fewer still may ever do so again. The intensity of his efforts and belief became so well known in New York that the term "Fullertonize" was adopted by his friends and business associates in order to describe his behavior, self-appointed mission, and style.

"The destiny of Long Island," he wrote toward the end of his life, "sees it the future crossroads of civilization, East and West. Blessed Isle!"[2] And, again, on a related occasion around the same time:

> Why is it the Blessed Isle? Why not. It lies in the frost belt of the temperate zone, yet has its short winters, mainly at night, above freezing by day, because Blessed by great guardian bodies of water North and South, because Blessed by more sunshine than all the rest of the U.S.A. except El Paso and Los Angeles which Uncle Sam rates a few hours more. Blessed, besides its pure air assured by its

guardian waters, it has absolutely pure water everywhere obtainable, inexhaustible in quantity, while protected from surface contamination by impervious strata of clays, in places kaolin of finest china making type.[3]

Photography played a critical role in this discovery process. Fullerton had come upon Long Island while seeking recreation and searching for subjects to explore with his camera. He soon became aware that in the course of enjoying his hobby, capturing scenes and recording events—preserving the visual texture and memory of places and activities, many of which were soon to change or disappear—he was casting and refining his own version of a tacitly-shared public vision and creating extremely useful tools with which to promote it.

Between 1890 and 1930 Hal B. Fullerton took, processed, collected, and used more than ten thousand photographs. Approximately 2,500 of his original glassplates and lantern slides were rescued from destruction in the late 1940s and donated to the Suffolk County Historical Society. Today, this collection comprises one of the premier visual archives for the study of Long Island history, landscape, economy, and social life. The images almost certainly represent Fullerton's best known and most enduring accomplishment.

This volume—and the exhibition it accompanies—began as an exploration of the photographs. It was evident from the onset of the investigation that the pictures could not be adequately understood or appreciated without reference to the career of which they were a part and the charismatic personality from which they emanated. Both Hal Fullerton and his "life partner" Edith were vibrant, emblematic figures of their age, whose lives and work were dedicated to the promotion of Long Island ideals and an ideal Long Island. To a large extent, at least initially, the focus of attention is biographical—to correct and augment the public record of the life and to clarify the motives surrounding the production, distribution, and consumption of the images. The perspective is also environmental, and the study devolves at least in part into a meditation on a very particular place (Long Island) and time (the turn of the twentieth century). Finally, there are technical issues—concerns with photographic method, style, popular visual convention, and influence. The images, then, provide access to a complex web of social, economic, and iconographic factors that were influential during a critical period of Long Island's development. In doing so, they are symptomatic of contemporaneous national trends in advertising, regional boosterism, and railroad-sponsored photography and promotion.

Fullerton's Early Years

The details of Fullerton's family background and early life are sketchy, since few original records from his past have apparently been preserved. According to all accounts, though, the boy christened Harry Barry Fullerton was born in Cincinnati, Ohio, on August 15, 1857, the first of three sons of William Reynolds and Frances Cornelia Lyon Fullerton. His father, later described as "a scion of Bostonese and Harvard nobility," had grown up in the Massachusetts capital and worked most of his life in the wholesale hardware business. His mother, he recalled, was "the fifteenth child of the French and Spanish pioneers of Cincinnati."[4]

He characterized his early education as "assorted, running from an abandoned back district log cabin, through *early Western* schools to the Massachusetts Institute of Technology and the University of Cincinnati."[5] Whether or not Fullerton ever actually attended the University of Cincinnati is uncertain. He did, however, enter M.I.T. in the fall of 1875, as a "regular" civil engineering student in the class of 1879, but only stayed for one year. This seems to have been less the exception than the rule, since only twenty-four of the original sixty-six regular class members actually graduated. The reasons for Fullerton's withdrawal are not well documented, but family tradition suggests that

M.I.T. Classmates "Sup" and Edward A. "Cutler" in tent, University of Pennsylvania campsite, during trip to Philadelphia Centennial Exposition, June 1876. Pencil sketch attributed to H. B. Fullerton. Courtesy, Ferguson Collection.

he was forced to leave college in order to help care for one of his parents, who had become seriously ill. His mother did indeed die around this time, after which his father moved to Holyoke, Massachusetts, where he subsequently remarried.[6]

At M.I.T., Hal Fullerton received practical scientific and mathematical training and developed drafting and graphics skills and an abiding interest in various forms of visual documentation and expression. His affiliation with "the Tech" always remained a matter of great pride to him.[7] He maintained contact with several school colleagues throughout his life, and actively served as an alumni officer of his class.[8]

One of the highlights of his year at M.I.T. was a visit by the entire student body (300 students in all) to the Philadelphia Centennial Exposition during June 1876—providing a timely introduction to the expanding wonders of American industry.[9] Fullerton's pencil sketches, diagrams, cartoons, and drawings that survive from this trip attest to his humor and skills as an observer and recorder and reveal his fascination with technology and the people and places around him.

Hal Fullerton was not a very large or muscular figure in person, but he projected a substantial, vibrant presence. He stood five feet seven, is remembered and depicted in photographs as being "permanently weather-tanned," with a gallantly upturned mustache, which whitened with age, as did his hair. He was full of energy, perpetually "wound up" and "on the move," seemingly boundless in his excitement and enthusiasms. As a natural talker and entertainer, his prose, in speech and writing, tended toward overelaboration and the humorous exaggeration of the tall tale. Drawing on the experiences of his youth, he cultivated an image of a "westerner," a former "cowboy," a man of action and practical knowledge, in much the same way as his contemporary, fellow Long Islander, and good acquaintance, Theodore Roosevelt. Underneath the brilliance and hyperbole of the boostering there were evident sincerity and a boyish attachment to naive, simple sentiments.

Between 1877 and 1886, Fullerton worked in a variety of industrial and commercial enterprises in Pennsylvania, Texas, Virginia, and Massachusetts. In 1877 or 1878, probably after spending time in Cincinnati, he turned up in "the oil fields" of western Pennsylvania, employed "as inside superintendent of an oil company."[10] Between late 1878 and the spring of 1880, he seems to have been in Texas, working as a "general utility man in a cotton seed oil mill," most likely the "H. O. Co."[11] (In later life he also spoke of adventures "as a cowboy on a ranch in the Dallas area" and a stint as a deputy sheriff.)[12] Some time during 1880–81 he also claimed to have worked as a hydraulic engineer for the Holyoke Water Power Company. In late 1881 he served as "assistant

The Office & No. 14, Oil Well, Western Pennsylvania, July 25, 1878. One of a series of pencil sketches by H. B. Fullerton, March 26–August 4, 1878. Courtesy, Ferguson Collection.

"The Man from Out West," Hal Fullerton in Mexican attire, c. 1892–93. Possibly self portrait or photograph by John Merritt, M. D. Courtesy, Ferguson Collection.

engineer" for the Canal and Water Power Division of the Richmond and Allegheny Valley Railroad, surveying for a dam constructed at Lychburg, Virginia. Returning to the Holyoke-Springfield area of central Massachusetts, where his father was living, he next spent four years "in the paper business on the New England circuit," most likely working for the Whiting Paper Company in Holyoke. Around 1886 he took a job as a "paymaster for a New England cotton mill." It was probably about this time that Fullerton married Mary Dwight Pierce, daughter of J. D. Pierce of Springfield, Massachusetts. The couple lived in Holyoke "for a number of years before removing to New York City."[13] Little more is known about Fullerton's years in New England or his first marriage.

Through his years of wandering, he became familiar with the workings of a variety of businesses and industries. He also developed an appreciation for a broad expanse of the American landscape and a sensitivy to regional traits and differences. In particular, he grew aware of the critical importance of railway operations and transport networks and the possibilities of the emerging fields of advertising and sales promotion.

In 1887, Hal Fullerton began a decade-long period of employment with the Seeger & Guernsey Company, international importers, exporters, and commission merchants, specializing in the trade of agricultural machinery and products with Mexico and Latin America. He first served as a buyer and manager, then assistant treasurer, and assistant secretary in the company's main headquarters in lower Manhattan. He was working in the New York office by August 1887 and continued to do so at least into 1890.[14]

During March 1890, Fullerton journeyed by train across Kansas, the Indian Territory (Oklahoma), and Texas, probably on business for the company. He may also have visited Mexico for a short period as

Caricatures of H. B. Fullerton, probably Texas or Oklahoma, c. 1890, artist unknown, Seeger & Guernsey Co. Courtesy, Ferguson Collection. These sketches offer a comic reflection on George Eastman's famous 1888 Kodak advertising slogan: "You press the Button, We do the Rest."

well.[15] It was also around this time that he became interested in photography.

He was back in New York by the spring of 1892. In June of that year he was given a major new assignment, as machinery manager of the Mexico City branch office, in which he was given authority to develop an aggressive advertising and publicity program.[16]

Fullerton arrived in Mexico City by August 1892 and remained there at least through February 1893.[17] While engaging in business, he traveled throughout the countryside, both taking and purchasing photographs and collecting antiquities, relics, and ethnographic specimens. He was particularly fascinated with the archaeological remains of the Aztec civilization and the Mayan ruins in the Yucatan. He returned to these images, objects, and experiences frequently throughout his later life, as they provided ample sources for reflection, elaboration, commentary, publication, and performance. (In 1896, he donated a large collection of his Mexican relics and antiquities to the Library and Natural History Museum in Springfield, Massachusetts,

Young Mexican girl grinding meal on quernstone, Mexico, c. 1892–93. Courtesy, Ferguson Collection.

where they remain today.)[18] If not precisely fluent in Spanish, he had a competent command of the language, which helped to familiarize him with local customs and establish a good rapport with his Latin American associates and customers. However, like most of the other North American businessmen, he seems to have socialized primarily within the small American colony in the Mexican capital. His wife had apparently passed away, perhaps in Mexico, more probably some time earlier—precisely when it is not clear.[19] It was during this Mexico City sojourn, however, that Hal Fullerton met the young Edith Loring Jones, who had come from Pennsylvania for a brief visit with her expatriate aunt and uncle, the Allens.

There was a nineteen-year age difference between Fullerton and Miss Jones; at the time of their introduction, she was sixteen and he, thirty-five. Yet the two developed a deep mutual affection, which endured a more than five-year, long-distance courtship.

Energetic, intelligent, engagingly attractive, self-assured, and talented artistically, Edith typified in many ways the emerging dynamic "new woman" of the 1890s. She had been born on Long Island, in Brooklyn, October 24, 1876, an only child of Quaker parents. After her mother's early death, she moved into the home of her maternal aunt and uncle in Bristol, Pennsylvania.[20] There she was raised within a pleasant extended family household, among female cousins close to her own age and several older, strong-willed Quaker aunts, who were deeply involved in local community affairs and philanthropic "good works." This setting probably reinforced Edith's attachment to liberal egalitarian ideals often associated with the Society of Friends, that is, valuing self-reliance, tolerance, freedom of conscience, and an active interest in social reform. It probably helped confirm her own sense of independence and familial dedication, and also her belief in the beneficence of nature and the importance of formal education and teaching, especially for girls and women. At the end of her Mexican vacation, Edith returned to the Jenkintown School from which she eventually was graduated. In the late 1890s, she moved to Brooklyn and entered Pratt Institute's recently established School of Kindergarten Training.[21]

In 1893 or 1894, Hal Fullerton transferred back to Seeger & Guernsey's New York office, where he continued to work for several more years as a company vice-president. Family tradition relates that he became seriously ill on his return from Mexico. According to one account, on arrival in New York it was discovered that he had contracted yellow fever as a result of assisting infected patients in a Vera Cruz hospital. After a period of quarantine, so the story goes, he was encouraged to take up bicycling as a form of physical therapy.[22] Whatever the extent of truth in this tale, it is certain that shortly after Fullerton came back to New York, he moved into the Brooklyn home of

Arverne—Cyclist Photographers on Beach, members of the Whirling Dervishes, Rockaway, 1897 (149.7.1172).

his good friend and physician, John Merritt.[23] Although the evidence is not conclusive, it seems that Merritt may have been in Mexico with Fullerton, as well.[24] "Doc" Merritt was an enthusiastic bicyclist, a founder of the Whirling Dervishes touring club, and also a devoted amateur photographer, a charter member of the Brooklyn Academy of Photography, and that group's president for 1893 and 1894.

Through or in association with his physician friend, Hal Fullerton became intensely involved in both these avocational pursuits. By the late nineteenth century, industrial and urban development had created opportunities for leisure and an immense appetite for new forms of recreation in America, especially among the middle and upper classes. The improved "safety" bicycle and the "Kodak" or box camera, twin products and symbols of the age, appealed to many of the same hobbyists. Bicycles provided a revolutionary means of independent locomotion and healthful open-air exercise, ideally suited for photographers' outings and club field trips. Bicycling also brought to widespread public attention the grossly inadequate condition of America's road system. Rutted, narrow, poorly graded and aligned, by turns muddy and dusty, most streets and thoroughfares were inconvenient, only seasonally usable, and little changed from their preindustrial condition.

Fullerton joined the Whirling Dervishes by the end of 1895, when he is known to have held the office of "cyclometer" (recording secretary) in the unique and eccentric cyling club, which was then two or three years old. (Typical of the exuberant good humor associated with the club—and Fullerton's own character—the officers were named for parts of a bicycle: "Crank Hanger" was president; Brake, first vice-president; Wrench, second vice-president; Pump, third vice-president; High Gear, captain; Sprockets, lieutenants; Tool bag, treasurer; Repair kit, surgeon; Cyclometer, recording secretary; Bell, bugler; and Lamp bracket, standard bearer.)[25] "Their purpose is road riding and touring, and incidentally . . . to become advocates of obedience to road rules, and promoters of courteous deportment among cyclists," according to an article on club activities in the *Brooklyn Citizen* of March 8, 1897.[26] Unlike the other Brooklyn cycling associations, which numbered forty-seven in 1896, the bohemian Whirling Dervishes were strictly "tourists" and did not maintain a clubhouse, have by-laws, or hold races.[27] There were 100 members, both men and women, in the Whirling Dervishes throughout the period of Fullerton's active involvement in the group, which extended from about 1895 to at least 1903. In 1897 most of the men were in their late thirties or early forties; the women averaged twenty-two years of age. Many of these fellow cyclists were dedicated amateur photographers.

Fullerton had also been a member of the Brooklyn Academy of Photography, the older of that city's two amateur photographic organizations. By the beginning of 1896, he was listed as the club's corresponding secretary. The Academy, which had been established in 1887 for "the advancement of photography in its scientific, historical, art and technical applications," had ninety-five active and fifteen corresponding members at the time.[28] The majority of the club's officers, and a good number of its members, were also, like Fullerton, active in the Whirling Dervishes and other local cycling groups.[29] Fullerton served as president of the Brooklyn Academy of Photography from 1897 through 1899; he remained active in the organization for several additional years.

Fullerton's interest in photography dated at least from 1890, when he apparently brought a camera on the railroad journey across Kansas. During his 1892–93 stay in Mexico, he photographed quite extensively, documenting Seeger & Guernsey's offices and warehouses; attempting landscapes, architectural and interior studies, views of archaeological sites and ruins, and ethnographic portraits.[30] Fullerton seems to have experimented with a variety of cameras and negative formats. Although no original negatives of the Mexican images are at present known to survive, large numbers of lantern slides and prints on platinum, solio, and albumen paper, evidently contacted from four-by-five-inch, five-by-eight-inch, six and one-half-by-eight and one-half-inch, and eight-by-ten-inch plates, are represented among the items still in the possession of his descendants.

In Brooklyn and on Long Island in the mid-1890s, Fullerton used almost exclusively a five-by-seven-inch view camera with glass dryplates. Just before the turn of the century, he also acquired a

Fullerton-Jones Wedding at Willowmere, Bristol, Pennsylvania, 1898, photographer unknown. Edith Loring Jones in Grecian wedding gown designed by H. B. Fullerton. Courtesy, Ferguson Collection.

mammoth eleven-by-fourteen-inch outfit, which he used to great effect. In the 1900s and 1910s, he made noteworthy use of both hand-applied image coloring techniques and autochrome plates, an early natural-color photographic process.

As an officer and active member in the Brooklyn Academy of Photography, Fullerton enjoyed exchanging technical information, discussing aesthetics, and exhibiting his own work and that of others. In the spring of 1901, for instance, he showed prints and lantern slides at the annual exhibitions of both the Academy (where he received a bronze medal and ribbon) and the photographic department of the neighboring Brooklyn Institute of Arts and Sciences (where he was awarded first prize for a flower study and additional prizes for lantern slides).[31]

Fullerton's life changed dramatically during 1897 and 1898. First, he left Seeger & Guernsey and began work for the Long Island Railroad (LIRR).[32] Then, the following year, the attenuated courtship finally ended. On June 3, 1898, he and Edith Loring Jones, then twenty-one years old, were married at the bride's family home, Willowmere, in Bristol, Pennsylvania. The pageantry of the event itself was carefully planned by the groom, in consultation with his bride, with typical exuberance and arts-and-crafts taste. He even designed the wedding dress, a simple, Grecian gown of cream-colored silk, which the bride herself made.[33] The lawn, house, and grounds of Willowmere were decorated with flowers and grasses specially chosen for the occasion. The groom's photographic record of the event, delicately printed on platinum paper, reveals a strong pictorialist influence.

After the wedding, the couple embarked on a honeymoon trip to Asheville, North Carolina, and en route stopped in Washington, D.C., where the groom also took some photographs. Travel was of course by rail, since Hal Fullerton could make privileged arrangements because of his new position with what would soon be a branch of the Pennsylvania Railroad system.

The marriage marked the beginning of a remarkable life partnership, in which husband and wife shared and contributed to

"Mira Flores" (See the Flowers) from the East across Lake Loring & the Island developed from the swamp which was sheep wash pond in olden times. Huntington, c. 1902–10. Courtesy, Ferguson Collection.

each other's work, interests, and creative endeavors. On their return to New York, the couple set up house in a rented apartment on Carleton Avenue in Brooklyn. There, on June 10, 1899, a daughter, Hope, was born.[34] Like most married women of her generation, Edith turned her attention at first to home and family life; she abandoned her studies at Pratt without completing a degree or graduating in the class of 1899. A little more than a year later, probably in early 1901, the family moved farther east, to a house in Hollis, central Queens, where, on February 10, 1902, another daughter, Eleanor Frances, was born.[35]

Desiring additional space for their growing family and inevitably attracted to more rural Suffolk County, six months later the Fullertons purchased an attractive, early nineteenth-century clapboard house on East Main Street in Huntington. They immediately commenced renovating and remodeling the house and grounds. The process of

Fullerton family, ice skates, and dog-harnessed pram on frozen Lake Loring, Mira Flores, Huntington, c. 1909. Courtesy, Ferguson Collection.

transforming the William J. Wood property into a residence and landscape of the Fullertons' own design was documented in photographs and feature stories in the Brooklyn and New York newspapers. The family remained deeply attached to "Mira Flores" (or, "See the Flowers"), as they named their homestead, in recollection of their Mexican sojourn.[36] Over the next eight years, as they developed the property further, especially the gardens, the Fullertons became involved in local community affairs. Hal, who served as secretary of the Huntington Horticultural Society, sponsored that group's first annual exhibition.[37] He documented with his camera the parades and pageants held during the town's 250th Anniversary Celebration, July 3–5, 1903.[38] In 1908 they became involved in local politics, when they petitioned their fellow "Loyal Huntingtonians," in an attempt to secure approval of a bond issue for the purchase and construction of new schools in the town.[39] Later that year, on May 24, a son, Loring, was born.[40]

Hal Fullerton took great pride and enjoyment in his family and home life. And, as had been the case with most of his personal interests and enthusiasms, they too became deeply involved in his work—as participants in his experiments, and exemplars of his ideals. Increasingly, too, after the turn of the century, Edith inspired and collaborated on these projects. In 1901, for instance, both he and his wife were active in organizing the Jamaica (Queens) Amateur Photographic Society.[41]

Cyclists' Paradise (Long Island City, 1897), H. B. Fullerton cover design, with winged cycle wheels.

Cyclists' Paradise

Fullerton seems to have been recruited by LIRR president W. H. Baldwin, Jr., specifically to help coordinate and enhance the railroad's efforts to encourage local road and highway improvements and to capitalize on the exploding mass market of recreational cycling. Baldwin, who assumed the presidency of the railroad following Austin Corbin's sudden death in a carriage driving accident in June 1896, had apparently known Fullerton through their joint involvement in the Good Roads Association (G.R.A.) of Brooklyn, an organization established in 1892 to promote grading, widening, and paving (macadamization) of thoroughfares in Brooklyn and nearby areas of Long Island, particularly "for the use of horsemen and wheelmen."[42] The initial object of the Association, which had in fact been organized by leading members of the Long Island Wheelmen and other Brooklyn cycling groups, had been the "building of smooth cycling paths from Prospect Park to Coney Island." The G.R.A. sought to lobby, fundraise,

Good Roads, Hard Beaches, and Ideal Paths, Brooklyn Cycle Club, Merrick Road, Lynbrook, 1897 (149.7.1223).

and secure locally what the League of American Wheelmen was performing on a national scale.[43]

Cycling underwent a phenomenal surge in popularity following the introduction of the rear-wheel-driven safety bicycle in 1885 and its improved form (with inflatable tires) five years later. There were only about 300 cyclists in Brooklyn in 1885; a decade later, an estimated 10,000 participated in the great Cycle Parade sponsored by the Good Roads Association to celebrate the opening of the Return Bicycle Path from Prospect Park to Coney Island.[44]

During 1896 and 1897, Fullerton played an increasingly prominent public role in cycling and transportation improvement circles. He was appointed one of the twenty Special Cycle Path Police for Prospect Park in May 1896, and served on the Good Road Association's five-man special Parade Committee for the Return Cycle Path opening festivities the following month. In 1897, he was elected to both the state board and national assembly of the League of American Wheelmen (L.A.W.) as a delegate from the second New York district

Cross Island Cycle Path, Patchogue to Port Jefferson, crossing railroad tracks, 1897 (356).

(for Long Island). He was also voted second vice-president of the Good Roads Association of Brooklyn and promoted and participated in the Brooklyn Cycle Show, held at the armory on Flatbush Avenue at Hanson Place in March, representing both organizations. Fullerton continued to serve as a delegate, officer, and committee head of the L.A.W. and the Good Roads Association for a number of years, gaining a national reputation as a vocal proponent of cyclists' interests and effective lobbyist for highway improvements during the 1900 presidential and congressional election campaigns.[45]

Shortly following his appointment as Special Agent of the Passenger Department for the Long Island Railroad in May 1897, Fullerton initiated several projects aimed at his expanding bicyclist constituency. Utilizing his experience in promotional writing, design, and printing, as well as his experience with the L.A.W. and G.R.A., he prepared his first publication for the railroad, *Cyclists' Paradise*, an attractive eighteen-page booklet, best described by its subtitle: "an accurate map showing only the ridable roads of Long Island with notes, suggestions, runs, hotels and time tables sufficient to enable any one to 'lay out a trip' intelligently." The booklet, which was available free of charge, outlined more than twenty recommended cycling routes on Long Island. The text begins with the premise that "every condition on Long Island is favorable to the cyclist" and notes that the Long Island Railroad "with its main line and many branches makes every portion of the Island easily accessible."[46]

To encourage and better serve the bicycling community, Fullerton arranged to have baggage cars equipped with special racks "to reduce the risk of damage to a minimum." As he boasted in the 1898 edition of *Cyclists' Paradise*, the Long Island Railroad "was the first to equip and run cars solely for transportation of bicycles." Fullerton's "combination passenger and bicycle car," fitted with League of American Wheelmen holders and hangers, was further refined and patented in June 1900, and then used by the New York Central and other railroads. Under Fullerton, the LIRR was also reputedly the first line in the world to run a "complete bicycle train," consisting of six of these special cars.[47]

The success of Fullerton's pilot efforts was noteworthy. During

Suffolk Co. Supervisors Coaxed to view Queens Good Roads, 1898 (149.7.1448).

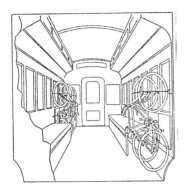

Handbill illustration for LIRR "Patent Combination Closed Passenger and Bicycle Car," which was "arranged to accommodate either passengers or bicycles in the same space by lowering the seats for passengers or raising them for bicycles," c. 1900. Courtesy, Ferguson Collection.

the summer 1897 season, the railroad carried 150,000 bicycles.[48] By October 1897, the first 10,000–issue printing of *Cyclists' Paradise* had been exhausted.[49] At least two subsequent editions appeared shortly thereafter; these also seem to have gone quickly out of print.

Unique Long Island

Among the particular attractions of Long Island noted in the *Cyclists' Paradise* was the claim that "for the artist and photographer prize-winning bits are on every hand."[50] Fullerton had combined his own interests in photography and cycling for a number of years prior to taking the position with the railroad. It was no doubt in the course of his involvement with the Brooklyn Academy of Photography that he conceived the idea of publishing an anthology of picturesque photographs as a promotional vehicle for the railroad.

The railroad had occasionally sponsored illustrated promotional publications since the 1870s. *Long Island and Where to Go; A Descriptive Work Compiled for the Long Island Railroad Company for the Benefit and Use of its Patrons*, a 262–page, paperbound volume, featuring picturesque wood engravings and advertising cuts, appeared in 1877. Issues of *Long Island Illustrated* appeared at least from 1882 through 1884 and another series, *Out on Long Island*, was produced between 1889 and 1892, or so. In the mid-1890s the railroad's traffic department was publishing and distributing at least two other booklet series, *Long Island by Sea and Sound (or, The Beauties of Long Island)* and *Summer Homes on Long Island*, both of which were illustrated with photographic halftones and artwork credited to the American Banknote Company. Even after Fullerton joined the railroad and had initiated his own publication program, the line continued to issue editions of *Long Island Illustrated* and *Summer Homes on Long Island* with old American Banknote Company photographs and some other revisions well into the early 1900s.

The first edition of *Unique Long Island* ("Illustrated from Occident to Orient by the Camera") was probably issued in the spring of 1898.[51] The 96–page booklet, offered "compliments of the Long Island Railroad Co.," contained 165 halftone reproductions of images taken on Long Island by H. B. Fullerton and twenty-five other amateur photographers, at least four of whom were members of the Brooklyn Academy of Photography. In contrast with the railroad's own earlier promotional publications—and most of those issued by other lines and resort areas during the same period—Fullerton's *Unique Long Island* utilized minimal text. As proclaimed on its title page, the book was

Easthampton—Some Summer Homes (Exclusive Row of Residences), c. 1903 (149.7.269).

presented "in the belief that the 'sun pictures' [photographs] will describe better than words LONG ISLAND'S many charms." The *Brooklyn Times* later praised the innovative nature of this concept: "There is nothing in the booklet of an advertising nature, with the exception of the photographs themselves. The only text in the book consists of the introductory title page, and the captions locating the scenes of the pictures. The photographs are allowed to tell their own stories."[52] The booklet presents both an enticing visual inventory of Long Island's advantages and "natural beauties," and a sampler of the categories or classes of typical advanced amateur imagery of the period—landscapes, marine views, snapshots, genres, architectural views, still lifes, and flower studies.

Although it is probably impossible to assess the effectiveness in

Long Island City, 65th Regiment, New York leaving James Slip for Camp Black (The First to Arrive at Camp Black. The First to Leave for the Front), May 1898 (149.7.1348).

market terms of Fullerton's approach, its appeal seems to have been immediate and dramatic. The railroad supported the annual publication of new editions of *Unique Long Island* for each of the next six years. A second, special 1898 issue credited the photographs to the same group of twenty-six amateurs; after this, all of the camera work can be attributed to the editor and designer, H. B. Fullerton. While he was never given the title of official photographer for the railroad, his job as Special Agent appears to have encompassed this area of responsibility.

Long Island's—and the railroad's—singular position during the United States' war with Spain, between April and August 1898, provided additional opportunities for Fullerton's photographic and public relations activities. Camp Black, on the Hempstead Plains, had been selected in the spring as the principal volunteer assembly point and training ground. In the summer, Camp Wyckoff, on the Montauk hills, was created for the yellow fever quarantine and recuperation camp for Theodore Roosevelt's Rough Riders and other troops returning from Cuba. The railroad naturally aided and encouraged the war effort, supplying critical transportation and depot services for men and supplies.

Embracing the intense jingoistic spirit of the times, Fullerton and the railroad commemorated the events in at least three special issues of *Unique Long Island*, published during or shortly after the war. The earliest volume, the Camp Black Edition, reprinted most of the illustrations from the first issue of *Unique Long Island*, supplemented by a selection of twenty-nine new images of the troops in transit and at the campsite. This booklet was "presented to the New York State Militiamen, their relatives and friends, as a souvenir of the campground upon which the New York Volunteers received the training that enabled them to astound the world by their deeds of valor, powers of endurance and high order of discipline."[53]

Two nearly identical editions, both subtitled "Bits of Beauty and Characteristic Sketches of the Island" and featuring "Two Great Spanish-American War Camps" followed, probably in the spring of 1899. In each of these 96–page booklets a revised introductory text page and a total of 183 halftones—49 images not found in the Camp Black volume, including 22 new halftones of photographs of Camp Wyckoff—are printed. Thus, the format for the series was well established before the turn of the century. Each subsequent issue began with a similar, short introductory page proclaiming Long Island's special qualities and the convenience and ease of railroad travel:

> Long Island is unique in every respect. Its natural beauties and perfect conditions are suited to every requirement. *Rest and Recreation, Sport and Pleasure, Agricultural and Industrial Pursuits*, and chief of all, *Healthy Homes* reached quickly and with comfort.
>
> The train service is first-class in all branches. New coaches, new parlor cars and new hard-coal burning engines have been added to the Railroad's equipment this year. Dustless road-bed, ballasted and oil-sprinkled. Fast express trains bring every section of the Island within easy reach of Greater New York.[54]

Fullerton's more recent pictures replaced or were intermingled with the earlier photographs. Familiar images sometimes reappeared in a different arrangement or order. Slight or subtle changes in layout or typography took place on occasion. After 1899 the number of informal snapshots and posed comic genres tended to decrease and finely detailed, deep-focused landscape, architectural, and marine views increase in number. Major revisions in both content and design were made for the

Company H., 71st New York. The First Tents Pitched at Camp Black. Hempstead Plains, May 1898 (149.7.1401).

33rd Michigan, Spanish War Veterans boarding ferry for home, L.I. City, August 1898 (149.7.1036).

1902 and 1904 editions. The underlying ideology and aesthetic remained essentially constant—Fullerton was promoting a convenient, traditionally "picturesque" environment for recreation, market gardening, estates, and suburban development.

Mile-a-Minute Murphy

Mile-a-Minute-Murphy in training, bicycling indoors on treadmill, Babylon, 1899 (149.7.1670).

In taking on the job as Special Agent for the Passenger Department, Hal Fullerton was encouraged by the railroad administration to do what came most naturally to him, which was to use his imagination to find ways to "advanc[e] the interests of Long Island" by promoting and advertising events, activities, or plans that would bring public attention to the Island's potential for sport, recreation, business, and residential development for both the middle classes and the urban elite.[55] One of Fullerton's earliest and probably his most dramatic attempts to capture the media spotlight and to gain widespread popular notice for the railroad was his promotion

Central Islip—LIRR Petroleum Dust-Subduer, rear view (Oiling the Road Bed), July 6, 1899 (149.7.1700).

of Charles M. Murphy's mile-a-minute bicycling run in 1899. Fullerton had known Murphy (1871–1950)—a champion amateur cycle racer and fellow Brooklyn resident—for a number of years through mutual involvement in the League of American Wheelmen and other local bicycling organizations.[56] The twenty-nine-year-old Murphy's desire to demonstrate that, in the absence of wind resistance, he could pedal a mile in one minute or under appealed to Fullerton's promotional instincts. (Murphy later claimed that he had been trying for thirteen years to interest other railroads in the project.)

The two collaborated closely on the scheme. Fullerton selected a two-mile stretch of level track at Maywood, on the Central line just east of Farmingdale. He also supervised the layout of a planked raceway between the rails and the design and construction of a special wind-protective hood to be attached to the rear of the pacing coach. Murphy undertook an elaborate, much-publicized training program, which Fullerton documented, along with the other aspects of the project, with his camera. Fullerton sent notices and invitations to all cycling publications and organizations, and made special arrangements to have members of the press from all sections of the country cover the event. After a nearly successful trial on June 21, during which Murphy rode the mile in 1:04.8, a final attempt was scheduled to coincide with the second day of the L.A.W. New York Division's mid-summer meet at Patchogue on June 30, 1899, for which the railroad also cleverly ran additional excursion trains.

With a crew of attending railroad officials, sports figures, timers, referees, and physician, Murphy raced the measured mile on his Tribune "Blue Streak" behind the locomotive pacer in 57.8 seconds. The sensational event, labeled by one cycling journal "by all odds the most remarkable performance ever made by a bicycle rider,"[57] was reported

Newsmen at work, preparing to document Charles M. Murphy's record-breaking ride, Maywood siding, Farmingdale, June 30, 1899 (149.7.1629).

Hal B. Fullerton testing the raceway for Murphy's run, June 1899. Photographer unknown (149.7.1216).

widely, much to Fullerton's satisfaction. Any significant positive impact the stunt may have had for the railroad is difficult to determine. It has been suggested that Murphy's interest in the project may have stemmed at least in part from a desire to investigate the aerodynamics of coach and rolling stock design. If, indeed, his intention was a serious test of this kind, it was not promoted as such. For Fullerton (and probably his superiors at the time), the wild public relations value—demonstrating the railroad's technical ingenuity and speed and its commitment to a large sporting constituency—was probably considered well worth the effort and expense. The event remained Murphy's most memorable accomplishment, which he recounted frequently, reenacted on the vaudeville stage in the early 1900s, and sought to repeat in his later years.[58]

Motoring

Fullerton's interest in technology, outdoor recreation, transportation and road improvements, and the promotion of Long Island's resource potential also brought his attention to developments in the new field and "sport" of automobiling. In December 1900 he was elected to the board of governors of the Long Island Automobile Club and appointed to the organization's "Good Roads" committee. At this same meeting, after the elections, Fullerton gave one of the photographically illustrated (lantern slide) lectures for which he had developed a reputation, on the subject of good roads.[59]

Motoring, associated at first with sports-minded men of exceptional wealth, many of whom could be attracted to the estate culture of the Island's expanding Gold Coast, was an ideal subject for such publicity treatment. On April 20, 1901, the Long Island Automobile Club sponsored—with Fullerton's encouragement and support—the first 100–mile auto endurance test in the United States. The course ran from Jamaica through Flushing, Manhasset, Port Washington, Roslyn, Oyster Bay, Massapequa, and Freeport to Hempstead. Fourteen vehicles, representing eight different manufacturers' machines, participated in the successful event, which received, thanks to Fullerton, widespread press coverage, including feature treatment in *Collier's Weekly*, as well motoring and "good roads" journals.[60] In a memorandum of congratulation, LIRR president William H. Baldwin found Fullerton's "advertising from such affairs" as the endurance test "undoubtedly a great benefit" to the railroad, and even supported his Special Agent's promotional activities much further afield, such as his efforts to establish a similar test course to Buffalo.[61]

Several months later, however, Fullerton's promotion of motoring had nearly fatal consequences, when he became a participant in one of the first collisions between a automobile and train engine in the United States. Fullerton's advice was often sought by sportsmen and reporters because of his intimate knowledge of Long Island geography and road conditions. In late October 1901, he was approached by an influential New York sportswriter colleague to help select a "proper place" where

A Transportation Convention—Coachman, Automobilist, Cyclist, Equestrian and Railroad—Mineola, c. 1901–02. Courtesy, Ferguson Collection.

noted French automobilist Henri Fournier could attempt a record-breaking straight-away mile run on a regular highway. Meeting in Jamaica on the morning of October 30, 1901, Fournier, Fullerton, and a party of four (two sportswriters and two auto enthusiasts) ventured out in Fournier's Mors French touring car through Queens into Mineola. Here they came upon millionaire motorist William K. Vanderbilt, who suggested one of his own favorite racing spots, on the Whale Neck Road just south of Westbury, for Fournier's run. After checking and approving this location, the group started back for Jamaica. Fullerton planned to return to the site later that day to measure the course and then arrange for official starter, timekeepers, and more extensive publicity; the race was scheduled for the following day. Driving across the main railway tracks at Westbury despite the warning signal and Fullerton's cautioning, the car encountered a detached eastbound locomotive on its scheduled run. The engineer cut his speed immediately, Fournier veered the auto off to the side, and all of the riders jumped out, except Fullerton, who was wedged in the front seat beneath his camera equipment and the driving levers. Whether or to what extent the train actually hit the car is not certain from the surviving accounts. All six riders were injured; three had to be taken to Nassau Hospital in Mineola. Fullerton's condition was the most serious; he was thrown from the vehicle, received head and leg injuries, and was knocked unconscious for three days. The auto ended up on the depot platform, a $12,000 loss. Needless to say, Fournier's speed trial was indefinitely postponed. By the end of November, though, Fullerton was well recovered and back to work. His interest in automobiles was only somewhat diminished. Three years later (in October 1904) he was busy publicizing and photographing the first Vanderbilt Cup race on the Jericho Turnpike.[62]

Photography, The Press, and The Lecture Circuit

During the half-decade following the Mile-a-Minute Murphy stunt, Fullerton's promotional activities for the railroad were constant and diverse. He became famous for his expertise in cultivating the press. In the summer of 1901, for instance, he was instrumental in organizing and publicizing the first Bay Shore Horse Show, which he saw as an opportunity to attract the metropolitan equestrian sports set to Long Island's South Shore. For the two-day event, held August 9 and

10, he had a special Pullman car run to transport the New York newspaper and magazine corps to and from the area. He supplemented this with extensive local arrangements, including free special stages, convenient accommodations, and receptions at the Penataquit-Corinthian Yacht Club. The event and the attendant newspaper coverage were considered extraordinarily successful.[63]

Throughout the period, photography remained central to his work, as to his avocational pursuits and interests. He traveled extensively about Long Island by train, bicycle, auto, and boat, documenting the events and scenes about him, as well as the railroad's own facilities and equipment, with both five-by-seven and more cumbersome eleven-by-fourteen glass-plate view cameras. *Unique Long Island* was just one of a large number of placement and publication outlets he utilized. Many of his images were reproduced often and usually in an assortment of print or projection transparency forms.

Fullerton early on established a reputation as an ebullient, captivating raconteur and public speaker. He probably began giving illustrated stereopticon talks around the time he joined the railroad; these entertainments soon became in great demand. In the fall of 1898,

Hal B. Fullerton, Medford homestead, c. 1915. Autochrome. Courtesy, Ferguson Collection.

for instance, he attracted a large audience for a lecture with views of Camps Black and Wyckoff at the Ferry Waiting Room in the Long Island Railroad YMCA branch, Long Island City. He followed this with another show entitled "Through Mexico, Cuba and Long Island" at the same location in April 1899. He often returned to entertain railroad employees here, as he did on February 25, 1903.[64]

He circulated with a lantern-slide lecture called "Unique Long Island," which he gave at the Fortnightly Club, Rockville Center, in November 1900, about the time he was also lobbying with a talk on "Good Roads." He gave presentations of his earlier, non-Long Island photographs, as well: illustrated talks on "Mexico," using images taken there during his 1892–93 stay, were apparent favorites, particularly in 1901, when he gave lectures on this subject at both the American Institute in Manhattan and Atlantic Hall, East Quogue.[65]

His repertoire was often humorous and idiosyncratic: he delivered an illustrated talk on "Bits of Unwritten History," at Columbia Hose Co. No. 1, Hollis, Queens, in April 1901. Fullerton prepared lantern-slide versions of much of his photographic negative work and presented lectures on most of the topics he treated in photo-

Edith L. Fullerton, Medford homestead, c. 1915. Autochrome. Courtesy, Ferguson Collection.

Illustrations from *Unique Long Island*, 1898–1904

Cranberry Pickers, Calverton-Riverhead, Immense Crops of Fine Firm Berries, 1897 (149.7.1550).

Shinnecock Links, Lady Champion, probably Miss Beatrice Hoyt, c. 1900–01 (149.7.43).

Firemen's Tournament, Sayville, 1899
(149.7.821).

Towards the Shipyards, Port Jefferson,
Jones Street, Port Jefferson, 1897
(149.7.1159).

Oystermen, Great South Bay, Off Blue Point (Dredging for Blue Points Near Patchogue), c. 1897–98 (149.7.1573).

Sorting Oysters, Blue Point-Sayville, c. 1897–99, with fellow Whirling Dervishes (149.7.814).

Lloyd's Harbor, Huntington, October, 1902 (149.7.295).

The Great South Bay—Blue Point, Shooting Ducks from Sunken Boat Blind, 1900 (149.7.26).

essay print form. When his duties with the railroad changed dramatically in 1905, he added new subjects and incorporated extensive new material into his talks. Fullerton continued on the slide lecture circuit into the late 1920s, several years past his official "retirement" from the railroad.

Beginning around the turn of the century, halftones and line renderings of Fullerton's photographs appeared regularly in the New York and Brooklyn press and in regional travel and sports periodicals. Both individual images, displayed prominently with captions, and illustrated feature stories, written by the photographer alone or in collaboration with his wife, were published. Picture spreads and articles ran in the *New York Commercial Advertiser, Brooklyn Times, New York Press, New York World, New York Herald* Brooklyn Supplement, the *Photo-American, New York Daily Tribune*, and the *Long Island Breeze* magazine.[66] Examples of his more distant placements include: *The Hub; Amateur Sportsman and Sportsman's Magazine;* the *Summer Travel Guide; Buffalo Illustrated Times; American Miller* journal, Chicago; *American Hay, Flour and Feed Journal; The Pointer;* and the *Boston Home Journal: An Illustrated Paper of Society and Travel.*[67]

By 1901–02, Fullerton had developed close connections and friendships with a number of important publishers, editors, and syndicated journalists in the New York area. He was on especially good terms with Julius Muller of the *New York Press* and McClure's Syndicate and with members of the F. N. Doubleday family and Walter Hines Page (of the New York and Garden City-based publishing company). Fullerton had in fact, at LIRR president Baldwin's recommendation, helped Page search for a suitable house and "country seat" on Long Island in 1901, shortly after Page and Doubleday formed their partnership.[68] Muller carried on a whimsical correspondence with the railroad agent and saw to McClure's syndication of Fullerton's humorous sketch about an unusual Christmas dinner in Mexico, "Abundio's Aztec Turkey," in December 1902 and probably other pieces, as well.[69]

Horticulture and Country Life

When Doubleday, Page & Co. brought out the magazine *Country Life in America* in 1902 and *Garden Magazine* three years later, it provided Special Agent Fullerton with convenient outlets for articles and photographs and encouragement to focus on a new subject area of personal interest—home gardening. *Country Life* ran numerous illustrated features by both Hal and Edith Loring Fullerton. These

Edith Loring Fullerton in Mira Flores garden, Huntington, c. 1903–05. Courtesy, Ferguson Collection.

included many pieces similar to H. B. Fullerton's other magazine placements, such as "The Snipe Archipelago," a short, humorous account of an outing to hunt shorebirds on Fire Island, which appeared in the June 1905 issue. There were, in addition, several series relating to vegetable and flower cultivation and landscape improvements at the Fullertons' Huntington home. The horticultural development of "Mira Flores" offered countless opportunities for experimentation, report, and analysis, during the course of which the couple refined their collaborative method. Edith became the principal writer; Hal conceived and produced the pictures. The articles, such as "The Best Salad Plants," which appeared in the May 1905 *Country Life*, through and beyond "Mowing the Lake" (on the transformation of "Sheep Wash Bog" into "Lake Loring") in the May 1910 issue of the same journal, offered a combination of amusing personal anecdote and practical suggestion with clear, often attractive halftone illustrations.

Many of these magazine pieces drew upon or supplemented material used by the Fullertons in their first major book-length

Eleanor Fullerton at rose arbor, Medford, c. 1914. Autochrome. Courtesy, Ferguson Collection.

collaborative work, *How to Make a Vegetable Garden: A Practical and Suggestive Manual for the Home Garden*. Doubleday, Page & Co. had commissioned and then published the work in April 1905, shortly after releasing a companion volume, *How to Make a Flower Garden*, an anthology of magazine pieces by several authors, including two articles and three pages of picture spreads by the Fullertons.[70]

How to Make a Vegetable Garden represents a substantial achievement and remains a valid and interesting work today. Written by Edith Loring Fullerton, the 367–page volume contains 250 detailed photographic illustrations by her husband, "The Man from Out West," to whom the work was also dedicated. The book was widely and favorably reviewed. The *Brooklyn Citizen* considered *How to Make a Vegetable Garden* "of much value to every one who has a country or a suburban place, whether large or small," while the *Eagle* found it one of the best works of its kind, "intensely practical," attractive, amusing, well-organized, gracefully written, illustrated, and designed.[71] The large number of photographs, documenting a wide variety of plant forms, their growth stages, and the minute steps in the gardening process, were frequently cited among the book's most outstanding features.

How to Make a Vegetable Garden epitomizes the mature Fullerton partnership style—pointedly didactic (or to use the period term, "instructive"), yet fundamentally personal and informal (by turns, quite often sentimental and humorous), presented through the sensitive interplay of text and visuals. The approach clearly reflects Edith's talents and suggests the influence of Progressive educational methods and philosophy and her experiences at the Pratt Institute

Long and short, fat and thin from "Roots We Eat," p. 221, in *How to Make a Vegetable Garden*. Courtesy, Ferguson Collection.

Real Sweet Potatoes and Plenty of Them, Wading River, 1906. Reproduced from 11–by–14–inch hand-colored glassplate transparency (189.19.5).

School of Kindergarten Training. There are charts, diagrams, maps, and detailed series of "planting tables." Family and friends are the characters; "Mira Flores," the setting. The method is homey; the message, progressive-romantic. The texture is probably best suggested in the author's own words. "It has been our earnest effort to tell the simple, necessary things, leaving the deep scientific parts to those who make such things their life-study," she notes in the Prologue. And in the Postscript adds:

> There are several marked advantages to be gained from possessing, planting and caring for a garden of one's own. First and foremost is the intimate acquaintance with Mother Nature, which must ever be ennobling, uplifting and broadening; secondly, a freshness and quality in one's food that is utterly unobtainable through any other source of supply; thirdly, a gain in health, if that be needed; and, last, but not least, the development of ingenuity, good sense and patience.[72]

The public appeal of this approach must have been obvious. By June 1907, Hal and Edith Fullerton were also writing and editing a "Half-Hour Gardening" feature for J. W. Muller and the McClure Newspaper Syndicate. While in Huntington, Hal Fullerton also applied his design and photographic skills to the promotion of suburban real estate development projects along the LIRR right-of-way. His 1905 pamphlet for the Matawok Land Company, which was apparently backed by a number of leading LIRR directors, used halftones from his *Unique Long Island* photographs to advertise property for sale in Newtown, Jamaica, Rocky Point, and Bridgehampton.[73]

Lure of The Land

The Fullertons' involvement in and promotion of scientific home gardening and horticultural education coincided with an important change in policy by the Long Island Railroad's management. Part of this new direction was, if not inspired by their work, then clearly reflective of it.

In 1900, the controlling interest in the line was obtained by the Pennsylvania Railroad, which simultaneously initiated plans for tunnel systems underneath the East and Hudson Rivers and a massive central terminal in Manhattan. The gradual creation, over the course of a decade, of a direct rail route across Long Island into Pennsylvania Station—McKim, Mead, & White's great "Temple of Transportation" in the city center—resulted in a rapid increase in commuter traffic.

In April 1905, in the midst of this ambitious expansion and modernization program, Ralph Peters was elected president of the Long Island Railroad. Peters, a southerner by birth and a long-term, second-generation railroad official, had previously served as General Superintendent of the Pennsylvania's Southwest System, west of Pittsburgh.[74] Cognizant of the Long Island Railroad's significant recent growth in passenger volume and anticipating further dramatic activity in this area in connection with the ongoing extension of electrification and the promised opening of through service to Manhattan, Peters directed his attention at seeking ways to increase the line's freight traffic. After a series of discussions and inspection tours with Fullerton and others, Peters became convinced that the railroad could both gain substantially and perform useful public service by actively promoting the scientific cultivation of the vast tracts of idle, "waste" land in northeast and central Suffolk County. The potential value of converting these 240,000 acres to productive agriculture had previously been recognized by railroad officials during the 1840s and 1860s, when several proposals were made to sponsor farm development. Folk traditions, however, probably militated against any immediate or sustained action, as did apparent lack of resources, technology, or concerted interest by the railroad.[75]

Ralph Peters, though, encouraged by Fullerton's support, "pioneer training" and spirit, seized upon the opportunity he perceived "to turn the whole country into good productive farms that would supply the New York market with fresh produce and incidentally . . . give the Long Island Railroad plenty of freight to carry all year round."[76] Within two months of assuming the presidency, Peters established an Agriculture Department for the railroad and appointed H. B. Fullerton as its head.

The role of the new department and Fullerton's immediate task as Director of Agriculture was to establish and oversee operations of an experimental farm, which would demonstrate the agricultural advantages and possibilities of Long Island, particularly the Suffolk pine barren and scrub oak "wilds." The position called for Fullerton's own particular combination of skills and interests as enthusiast and facilitator, photographer, amateur scientific agronomist, publicist, and showman. The object of the plan was to convince by "practical demonstration." Each step of the process was to be meticulously documented—photographed, measured, and recorded. Quantification was essential. Individual work diaries and a daily weather report, conducted under U.S. Government regulations, were also carefully maintained. The results of the work—the produce, pictures, facts, and figures—were to be continuously brought to public attention and made available for inspection by experts and the press on a regular basis.

A number of railroads in the United States and Canada were beginning at this time to undertake similar large-scale, organized development and marketing programs. In addition to having separate departments and publications to advance tourism and leisure travel, as the Long Island Railroad had had for several decades, many lines were forming divisions and hiring specialists to foster general publicity; "colonization" and "immigration" (particularly to thinly populated areas in the West, mountains, and plains); and industrial, real estate, and agricultural development. By 1906 these programs had become so prevalent that a national organization, the American Railway Industrial Association, was formed to share information and coordinate activities. (Naturally, both Hal and Edith Fullerton became leading figures in this organization, which was later known as the American Railway Development Association, or A.R.D.A.)[77] The Long Island Railroad's Agricultural Department was probably not the first established by an American railroad, and Peters may have made his decision with the experience of another line or branch of the Pennsylvania system in mind.[78] Fullerton's program was, however, one of the earliest, most ambitious, and best-publicized in the country, and its operation clearly helped engender many similar efforts elsewhere.

Peters's instructions—and challenge—of August 1905 were simple: "Find the worst ten acres on the north shore upon which to establish Experimental Station No. 1." Hal Fullerton undertook this new charge as a team effort with his wife and "full partner" (as they called each other), Edith Loring. Together they located and he photographed two potential plots of "waste land" along the North Shore Division of the railroad, which were then reviewed by President Peters. An eighteen-acre parcel at Wading River, which they had been assured "was the 'no goodest' piece of land to be found," was selected

Hope Fullerton Packing Home Hamper, probably Medford or Wading River, c. 1912. Courtesy, Ferguson Collection.

and purchased by August 19; preliminaries were settled by August 23. Conferences on clearing and site development followed. Ten acres were intended for the market garden; the additional eight would provide for an experimental dairy.[79]

Commuting from their Huntington home, the Fullertons began work at Wading River on September 1 by mapping out the house lot and establishing camp for an initial four-man local crew. This group was almost immediately replaced by a larger gang of Italian immigrant laborers, whose job it was to clear the brush, cut and set aside cord wood, and burn the scrap branches and ground. Hal Fullerton devised what was then considered innovative worker housing for his woodsmen by requisitioning, moving, and then adapting two condemned railroad freight cars for the site.[80]

Adopting another unusual method, dynamite was used for clearing stumps. Blasting commenced on September 6, an event observed by the invited "editors of all the big New York and Brooklyn daily newspapers and many editors of the prominent magazines."[81] After each series of explosions, the stumps were burned and the ashes spread over the ground as fertilizer. This method of clearing proved to be extremely cost-effective and added nitrogen to the soil. Local residents, however, commented disparagingly: "Aw they're plantin' dynamite and raisin' hell, and that's all they ever will raise."[82]

The "Junior Partner" Blowing Stumps By Battery, Wading River, 1905. Reproduced from *Lure of the Land* (1912).

Well drilling started in mid-October and was completed by the end of the month. After only 64½ working days from the start of clearing, the Fullertons proudly reported, the ten-acre market garden plot had been "cleared, plowed, disc harrowed, cross harrowed with a spring tooth harrow and drilled with rye."[83]

During November, a five-room portable bungalow, two seasons old, acquired from a South Shore beach, was moved to the site and reerected on a new foundation as the farm supervisor's cottage and adminstrative office. Clearing of the dairy plot continued. Paths and drives were constructed, fencing set, a water tower and tank system built, and hedges and nursery orchard stock planted over the winter months.

By the end of the summer of 1906, in the course of less than a year, the farm had already attained a remarkable level of productivity. In July, the first experimental "home hampers," specially designed and prepared crates containing baskets of fresh produce, which were packed at the farm and shipped by rail direct to consumers, were

Baskets of strawberries for the Hotel Seville, Medford, c. 1907–22. Reproduced from 11–by–14–inch glass (positive) display transparency, hand-tinted by Edith L. Fullerton (189.29.2).

Front and back covers for *The Lure of the Land* by Edith Loring Fullerton (Long Island: Long Island Railroad, 3rd edition, 1911). Hal Fullerton and daughter Hope appear on the front cover; daughter Eleanor, author Edith, infant Loring, and Hope are shown on the back cover (149.7.513–14).

successfully tested. This method of mail-order marketing without the intervention of a commission merchant was viewed by Fullerton as a critically important new concept. Using the slogan "Farm to Family— Fresh," he promoted the "home hamper" as an innovation of national significance, a key to creating a new system of urban food supply in America. The first season's promotional tours culminated on August 7, 1906, with a scheduled visit by agricultural experts and educators, who were treated to a special dinner of the farm's products, including ten different vegetables.

Before the end of the first year in operation, there were 380 varieties of cultivated plant life flourishing at "Peace and Plenty," as the Fullertons named the experimental station. The farm succeeded in producing 180 types of vegetables, 64 of fruits and berries, 19 kinds of forage, and 117 varieties of foliage and flower plants.[84]

To publicize the accomplishments, Fullerton had a portable exhibition building constructed, which he took to both the Riverhead and Mineola Fairs in September. As the *Riverhead News* enthusiastically described it:

> The building was filled with photographs and vegetable exhibits, the photographs accurately depicting the work done at the experimental farm from the time the rushes were cut down to the harvesting of the crops. Beside the exhibits in the house the vegetable hall contained a number of exceedingly good vegetables of every description grown by Mr. Fullerton this summer, showing that Long Island's poor soil will certainly produce good crops if the proper methods are applied.[85]

Immediately afterwards, with the experience of *How to Make a Vegetable Garden* behind them, the Fullertons refashioned their material into printed form. An illustrated leaflet, *Reclaiming Waste Lands on Long Island: Two Hundred Thousand Acres Available Which Can Be Easily Cleared of Trees by Dynamite and Cultivated by Simplified Modern Methods* previewed selected text and images. *The Lure of the Land: A Call to Long Island*, a 160–page, hardbound volume, written by Edith Loring Fullerton, with photographs by her "senior partner," was published by the railroad in late 1906. The work is an extraordinarily clever, convincing, and well-crafted piece of promotional literature, in which informal narrative, scientific observation, statistics, cost analyses, and testimonial are interrelated with straight documentary botanical and landscape views and picturesque or humorous genres and portraits. The book's effectiveness and charm are closely tied to the fact that the characters and events depicted in the text and illustrations are all identified as family, friends, and associates of the narrator-author and the photographer. The message, manner, and mode of presentation are all personal, aimed at a broad popular audience. The method simply builds on the approach used to promote gardening at Mira Flores.

As with his earlier publicity work, Hal Fullerton also took this picture-story on the lecture circuit. He was giving lantern-slide presentations on the farm's progress throughout the metropolitan area by the beginning of 1907. "Three Hundred Eighty Varieties of Vegetables" was the topic of one such talk given for the Stewards' Association of New York at the Columbia Club on Lexington Avenue. As the *Port Jefferson Echo* reported on February 7, 1907, "H. B. Fullerton, the 'Luther Burbank' of Long Island, said that it is not necessary to import fancy vegetables from foreign countries, as they could be raised on Long Island." Among the 380 plants successfully cultivated at the experimental farm in the first year, he had grown "many of the fancy salad and other vegetables which are usually imported."

The Littlest Girl and the All-Head Cabbage, Eleanor Fullerton at the Wading River farm, as depicted in *Lure of the Land,* 1906. Reproduced from vintage lantern slide. Courtesy, Anne F. Nauman Collection.

Stand with berries and vegetables, c. 1915. Autochrome (149.7.2220).

To further capitalize on the promotional momentum gained from Peace and Plenty's first year in operation, and to sway criticism that the success could not be duplicated on the lighter, sandier, poorer soils in the center of the Island, Fullerton established a second demonstration farm in early 1907. Eighty acres "containing the worst ten acres on the main line" were purchased by the railroad at Medford, fifty-two miles east of New York City for the Agricultural Department's Experimental Station Number Two, dubbed "Prosperity Farm." The ten acres for the market garden were cleared using the same methods developed at Wading River; the portable exhibition building used at fairs was moved to the homestead plot for the manager's house and office; a well was driven, tower and barn built, and planting begun before spring.

By the summer of 1907, the full extent and ambition of Fullerton's Agricultural Department had begun to be realized. Not only were there two experimental stations to manage; there was also an extremely active publications office to run.

The Lure of the Land had attained widespread popularity and succeeded in generating extensive correspondence. A full-time secretary was assigned to the department, which operated for the first

Edith L. Fullerton packing tomatoes, Wading River, c. 1906. Reproduced from 11–by-14–inch glass (positive) display transparency, hand-tinted by Edith L. Fullerton (189.29.1).

three years out of makeshift quarters, the "Hayloft" office, in the Fullertons' barn at Mira Flores. In response to the increasing requests for information about the project, LIRR president Peters proposed that a "leaflet" be issued at regular intervals to provide interested readers with reports on the progress of the demonstration farms. The Fullertons obliged by producing the *Long Island Agronomist*, "a fortnightly record of facts together with deductions based upon nature's practical demonstrations," the first number of which appeared on July 31, 1907. Issues were offered free of charge upon request. From an initial subscription list of about 600, distribution expanded to 7,500 within three years. By 1914, when it suspended publication, the journal was reaching approximately 16,000 subscribers worldwide.[86]

The *Agronomist* was published every two weeks until the end of 1909, when the cumulative demands of farm management and the burden of editorial production "made a less frequent issue a necessity" and the journal became a monthly.[87] The continuous stream of publicity increased demand for *The Lure of The Land*, as well. After the initial (1906) run became exhausted, the Fullertons

Loring Fullerton in field of alfalfa, Medford, c. 1913. Reproduced from 11–by-14–inch hand-colored glass-plate transparency (189.24.4).

Medford—Homestead at Experimental Farm No. 2, c. 1907 (149.7.436).

revised and expanded the work. The second, enlarged edition was issued in 1909; two others followed, in 1911 and 1912.

By the spring of 1910, the strain of commuting and dividing time among Huntington, Medford, and Wading River had become too much for the growing family. The Fullertons had spent three of their last four summers at the experimental farms—the 1906 and 1907 seasons at Wading River, and 1909, in Medford. The birth of a son, Loring, in May 1908, had barely provided a temporary pause in this frenzied schedule.[88]

Initially, the operation of the LIRR Experimental Station No. 2 had been conducted "by voluminous written instructions and long distance telephone." By the spring of 1909, however, it became apparent that more direct, personal supervision was necessary. Two portable buildings—one with five rooms, the other with two—were purchased and installed for the Fullertons and for guest quarters.[89] In June of the following year they left Mira Flores for good and took up permanent residence for both themselves and the *Agronomist* publication office at

Prosperity Farm. The journal's June 1, 1910 issue (volume 3, number 16) was the last to be produced from the Huntington barn-office. By the next month's number (volume 3, number 17), which bore the banner notice, "Publication Office, Medford, Long Island," the Fullertons were settling into what became known as The Homestead at "the Farm."[90]

With the move to Medford, Hal Fullerton became engrossed in the life and work of the Farm. Since about 1905, the focus of his publicity efforts and personal attention had gradually shifted away from the broad canvas of Long Island's many "wonders" toward the more intimate portrayal, by specific example, of the region's potential as model home-and-market garden. Medford provided the opportunity to extend the microcosmic treatment developed with Edith at Mira Flores.

At the Farm, Hal B. Fullerton, A.E. (agricultural expert), adopted a

Col. Roosevelt, President Peters, Mr. and Mrs. Fullerton, Wading River, August 10, 1910. Photographer unknown (149.7.1705).

61

Home Hamper with vegetables, c. 1906–09. Hand-colored lantern slide (149.7.2216).

Peaches on ledge, c. 1915. Autochrome (149.7.2213).

new persona, something akin to a "squire," as he presided over the experimental station, espousing progressive ideas, dispensing advice, and demonstrating scientific methods.[91] He and Edith sought to teach by practical example, to develop models of economy, efficiency, and spirit. As a family with three growing children, the Fullertons were deeply concerned with the development and improvement of the educational and social amenities within the incipient Medford community. Largely through the Fullertons' efforts, a new schoolhouse, polling place, Grange Hall, and library were added to the village between 1910 and 1917.[92] The establishment of the Grange chapter (Medford Grange, Patrons of Husbandry No. 1324) provided an effective local forum and group purchasing network by which to extend the work of the Farm.

A month after moving to Medford, Hal Fullerton invited ex-President Theodore Roosevelt to visit in order to help publicize and certify the experimental farm program. Fullerton, of course, viewed himself as a Progressive in the Roosevelt mold, and in 1912 supported the former president's independent party bid for reelection.[93]

The visit on August 10, 1910, was choreographed as a media event in typical Fullertonian fashion. Roosevelt was provided with the LIRR president Peters's special train (to which extra press cars were attached) for the trip. At Medford, TR was escorted to the Homestead, which had been just been hastily finished for this event. Here, he was treated to the first meal prepared in the Fullertons' new quarters. Later that afternoon, the party took off by automobile (an IHC, manufactured by the International Harvester Company), Edith Fullerton driving, to the Wading River farm. The memorable outing was photographed by Fullerton and covered in the New York press.[94] The choice of driver was of course conscious and symbolic of Hal Fullerton's style, method, and belief in another vital, timely Progressive cause—equal rights and

Fruit Crate (Home Hamper) with apples, peaches, and grapes, c. 1915. Autochrome (149.7.2221).

opportunities for women. For, despite his "Western" swagger and somewhat patriarchal manner, Hal Fullerton professed a dedication to equal partnership marriage and encouraged the self-reliance, advanced education, and independence of his wife and daughters. He also supported the women's suffrage campaign, in which Edith Loring Fullerton became involved in 1914–15, through her Grange activities and work in the agricultural education reform movement. Addressing a countywide suffrage worker convention in Patchogue on May 30, 1914, Edith Fullerton called upon farm women to develop strength, competency, and business skills in scientific farming, home management, and child care. "Every intelligent woman," she remarked, "is a suffragist at heart."[95]

The opening on September 8, 1910, of the direct rail route between Medford (and all of central Suffolk County) and the newly completed Pennsylvania Station lent added importance to the Fullertons' mission. Over the next four years, they immersed themselves in farm activities and expanded their promotional efforts through additional lectures, exhibitions, and publications. The production of small fruits—raspberries, gooseberries, currants, grapes, strawberries, peaches, apples, and Japanese plums—became a specialty of the Medford farm, which eventually came to produce "nearly 1,000 varieties of plants from many sections of the globe," including many exotic, nonwestern species of vegetables.[96] Experimental dairy operations also attained considerable success by 1912–13.

Both Hal and Edith Fullerton made frequent public appearances to discuss the work of the farms and advance the cause of agricultural

Baskets with apples, c. 1915. Autochrome (149.7.2212).

education. In April 1910, for instance, Edith Fullerton addressed the Women's Agricultural Congress at Bryn Mawr, Pennsylvania, describing the success of the two LIRR experimental stations. Similarly, Hal Fullerton spoke before classes at the Connecticut Agricultural College at Storrs and many other schools and professional groups.[97] Through the *Agronomist*, the Fullertons lobbied successfully for the establishment of local Farmers' Institutes by the Cornell Extension Service and ultimately the creation of Long Island's own agricultural college, the State Institute of Applied Agriculture at Farmingdale, which finally opened in 1916.[98]

With her training in early childhood education, Edith Fullerton naturally sought to involve her own and other school-age children in farm work and horticultural reform. Throughout the 1910s, she and Hal collaborated on articles, books, and pamphlets specifically for young children. Continuing the humorous, informal style and tradition of *How to Make a Vegetable Garden*, they produced *Small Gardens for Small Folks*, a thirty-one page paperback booklet, which the W. Atlee Burpee seed company published and distributed in 1912. While authored by Edith Loring Fullerton, the pamphlet was in effect a family endeavor. It is dedicated "with all a mother's love to my Chiquitas, 'Mousie' [Hope] 'Pigeon Pie' [Eleanor] and 'Sunny Jim,' [Loring]" and contains illustrations "from actual photographs of 'my chiquitas' as they were 'snapped' happily at work in their gardens by their Father The 'King of Our Castle.' "[99] A series of similar, but more extensive, illustrated articles entitled "The Child's Garden" appeared in the *Country Gentleman* magazine several years later. These were subsequently assembled, with an introduction by Arthur S. Dean, into *The Book of the Home Garden*, which was published by D. Appleton and Company in 1919.[100]

Through the *Agronomist* and the demonstration stations the Fullertons also initiated three Young Folks Clubs—one each for Corn, Potatoes, and Cauliflower. Offering annual cash prizes for complete crop reports for the cultivation of quality produce, the clubs for boys and girls under twenty-one anticipated the better-known 4–H movement by a number of years.[101]

As fairs, expositions, and trade shows became more common and popular in the decade preceding the First World War, the activity of the Agriculture Department's exhibition program increased dramatically. In addition to the appearances, each fall, at the Suffolk County (Riverhead) and Queens-Nassau County (Mineola) Fairs, where the produce were regularly awarded prizes and the displays attracted considerable interest, Fullerton sought more distant and prestigious venues and greater exposure for the exhibits. At the 1906 Exposition International in Milan, Experimental Station No. 1 was awarded a bronze medal for the "rapid, cheap and common sense method of

LIRR Agriculture Department Display, New York City Land Show, probably Madison Square Garden, c. 1912 (149.7.490).

Advertising pamphlet issued by The Larrowe Milling Company, Detroit, Michigan, 1913. Courtesy, Ferguson Collection.

clearing undeveloped territory" for agricultural development.[102] Fullerton used a variety of novel exhibit techniques, combining live and freshly picked produce, photographic prints, explanatory placards, maps, and unusual eleven-by-fourteen-inch back-lit, hand-tinted glassplate photographic transparencies. Prior to 1910 the farms won prizes (including the highest awards) at both the American Institute and the Horticultural Society in New York City. Displays were brought to the New York State Fair at Syracuse in September 1911. That same and the following year, the Fullertons participated in the two spectacular Land Shows—major development exhibitions of the agricultural, mineral, and forest resources of the United States and Canada—held in New York City. Despite extravagant competition, the railroad's farm displays succeeded in winning several prizes at both Madison Square Garden (1911) and the Seventy-first Regiment Armory (1912). Edith Fullerton took immense pride in the fact that her experimental farm "scrub cow" butter was awarded a gold medal at the 1912 New York State Fair and a bronze at the 1913 National Dairy Show in Chicago.[103]

Expansion of the Agricultural Department came to an end in 1914. On March 31, the Wading River farm, Experimental Station No. 1 ("Peace and Plenty"), closed and all operations were transferred to Medford.[104] Seven months later, the *Agronomist* ceased publication.[105] This retrenchment was justified and supported by the Fullertons themselves. Their promotional efforts had helped inspire the creation of other organizations and agencies to supply many of the farms' original educational and support services. Cooperative projects were now possible with the local Grange chapters, the farmers' institutes and State extension courses, new county farm bureaus, and the recently chartered, developing agricultural college. One of the last issues of the *Agronomist*, for example, incorporated the first number of the *Long Island Tryst* by the Bureau of Information and Markets of the Suffolk County Pomona Grange.[106]

The Medford Farm remained a vital component of the railroad's development and promotional effort well into the 1920s. LIRR president Peters, who believed strongly in the "need of increasing the food production not only of Long Island, but the Nation as well," continued to support the Fullertons' work and encouraged their participation in public discussions of national economic and agricultural issues.[107] The outbreak of war in Europe brought renewed attention to questions of American preparedness, self-sufficiency, and the cost and allocation of essential resources. Toward the end of 1914, Hal Fullerton served on the National Municipal League's committee on "The relation of the city to its food supply."[108] Around the same time, Edith Fullerton was a featured speaker at a Philadelphia women's organization conference analyzing "the high cost of living," particularly the differences in food and produce prices as experienced by the farmer and the household consumer.[109]

The Great War

In 1915 Ralph Peters offered the railroad's services and facilities to the army in the event of wartime need. Hal Fullerton proposed an area in eastern Suffolk between Yaphank and Manorville as a potential military training center. These suggestions were adopted after war was declared in April 1917. Two massive camps were established along the railroad lines. "Camp Long Island," later rechristened Camp Upton, was hastily constructed in June on the Yaphank site selected by Fullerton. In August, Camp Mills was opened on the site of old Camp Black on the Hempstead Plains. When the railroads were taken over by the U.S. Government in December 1917, Ralph Peters was appointed Federal Manager of the Long Island System.[110]

During the war period the railroad handled more than 3 million troops "on 5,984 special trains under Government orders" and almost 1 million tons of freight for military purposes. Approximately three-quarters of the U.S. Army in Europe is believed to have encamped on Long Island. The railroad was involved in the critical transport of troops and materials among the two major camps; the Roosevelt, Mitchel, and Hazelhurst air fields; a small naval base at Montauk; and the metropolitan district Army Supply Base in Bay Ridge.[111]

To aid the homefront effort, the railroad organized the Long Island Food Reserve Battalion, in which the Fullertons and the Medford demonstration farm participated. The Battalion operated a "Food Preservation and Instruction Train," which traveled across the Island during May 1917, providing literature, recipes, lectures, and canning demonstrations. Edith Fullerton served on the committee in charge of the project and as one of its principal instructors. The Battalion also assisted in the distribution of seeds, fertilizer, and nursery stock, and acted as a clearinghouse for the procurement of farm labor and machinery.[112]

In addition to these and the regular activities at the Medford Farm, Edith Fullerton operated a canning kitchen for the railroad men who ran the trains into and out of Camp Upton and offered volunteer service at the recuperation hospital. She washed and reworked gauze compresses and surgical dressings, visited the patients often, providing specially prepared baskets of fruit and biscuits, and even devised physical therapy (embroidering) projects for the ailing soldiers. It was during the war years that Hal Fullerton became involved in the Boy

Chief Grub Scout, probably Medford, c. 1917. Courtesy, Ferguson Collection.

Scout movement. After organizing a troop for his son and the other boys in Medford, he served as scoutmaster, commissioner, and inaugurated a national victory garden program, from which he assumed the proud title of "Chief Grub Scout."[113]

The Great War marked a quiet turning point in Hal Fullerton's life and career. Entering his sixties and commencing his third decade of service with the railroad, he had gained a national reputation as an agricultural expert. The children were growing up, going away to school, starting careers and families of their own. The ongoing maintenance and development of the Medford Farm remained demanding tasks. Opportunities for dramatic innovation were, however, limited. The experimental station had become part of a larger network of agricultural support and information services on Long Island.

Fullerton's promotional and photographic methods had also begun to change during the war period, as he responded to the availability of new technologies and materials. He had always felt the inadequacy of monochromatic imaging to portray the horticultural potential and wonders of his Blessed Isle. For years, he had depended on Edith's elaborate hand coloring to enliven the photographic prints, projection slides, and backlit display transparencies in his exhibits and presentations. When the Lumiere or autochrome plate—the first successfully marketed, practical color process—finally became available, Fullerton quickly jumped at the chance to produce direct, natural-hued photographs. He made autochrome lantern slides, which he had commercially finished, from about 1914 into the mid-1920s.

At the same time that he was experimenting with color, he abandoned his eleven-by-fourteen-inch camera outfit and turned from glassplate negatives to smaller format flexible nitrate film. After 1920, he became less conscientious about his photographic work, although he continued to document the farm's operations, produce, and exhibits. He also encouraged others, including his daughters, to take pictures. The railroad utilized many other photographers and publicity men in its promotional efforts.

After the armistice and demobilization, the Long Island Railroad was restored to private ownership in December 1919. The following spring, as the Fullertons were preparing to embark on a series of experiments in sugar beet cultivation, they were approached by the American Committee for Devastated France, requesting assistance in the effort to reestablish the agricultural areas along the Belgian border. Anne Morgan (J. P. Morgan's sister and the head of the volunteer group) came to recruit Hal Fullerton because of his reputation as a commonsense scientific farm specialist, who understood the effects of explosives, having successfully "dynamite plowed" the Long Island pine barrens. The Committee hoped to advance the resettlement and restoration of the Aisne region, which many French government officials considered to have had become uninhabitable.[114]

Securing a leave of absence with the railroad and turning over the farm operations to his wife and partner, Hal Fullerton set out for France in late April 1920. He was accompanied by his eighteen-year-old daughter Eleanor, who took a three-month break from her junior year at the Ambler (Pennsylvania) School of Horticulture for Women to serve as his secretary and assistant.

The Fullertons' assignment for the Committee was threefold: to assess the extent of damage to the ancient agricultural section and suggest methods of reclamation; to document their work for the official record and promotional purposes; and to introduce simple American labor-saving farm tools and equipment to the region. During the well-publicized trip, they toured and photographed the trenched battlefields and ruined villages of the former "No Man's Land," met with French agricultural experts, and cleared and developed sections of a two-acre demonstration kitchen garden plot near the Committee's headquarters in Blerancourt. Hal Fullerton's appraisal of the battle zone soil conditions proved to be reassuring to the French officials, who had held the exaggerated view that the land had been virtually ruined. Fullerton recognized that the critical task facing the French was an "engineering job," rather than an agricultural one. He noted that the subsurface soil had actually been enhanced by the bombing, which had added nitrogen and pulverized limestone. Ironically, the land had been "fertilized by the waste of war." After "clearing away the war wreckage, filling these trenches and shell holes, smoothing everything into fields

Foyer Civique, entrance to head-quarters of American Committee for Devastated France, Bleran-court, Aisne, France, 1920. Courtesy, Ferguson Collection.

once more," he commented, "[the] soil will respond with crops far better than it ever raised before."[115]

Without the heavy motorized equipment needed for more extensive grading, the Fullertons prepared their small, sample garden parcel by hand, demonstrating the use of the "Planet Jr." adjustable wheel hoes they had brought for this purpose. Their modest mission completed and reports and pictures filed, the Fullertons left France for New York at the end of June. Articles about the project, illustrated with their photographs, appeared in a number of periodicals and daily press rotogravure sections.[116]

Final Years

On his return to Medford, Hal Fullerton resumed his campaign to promote sugar beet production on Long Island. He had first grown sugar beets at Prosperity Farm in 1912, but since the war had come to see the crop as a resource of enormous economic potential.[117] Fullerton was convinced that Long Island's soil and climate were ideally suited for sugar beet culture. Furthermore, he noted, "there is enough available land . . . to support about 30 large sugar factories capable of a combined yearly output of some 350,000 tons," all, he proposed, within easy reach of the enormous New York market.[118] Between 1920 and 1926, Fullerton lobbied relentlessly for the establishment of a sugar factory, as the Agricultural Department sponsored annual sugar beet growing contests, offering sweepstakes and awards for quality and percentage of sugar, as well as raw tonnage. The industry, however, never materialized, and the campaign came to an end as the railroad began phasing out its farm program at the end of the decade.

Edith Fullerton, who by 1915 had been officially designated Assistant Director of Agriculture, shared responsibility for the Farm's management. During the 1920s, she worked closely with the Grange and Home Bureaus, taught household efficiency, and promoted the modern design and layout of farm kitchens.[119]

By 1925, when the Farm attained its peak level of production and diversity of crops—growing "more than 1,000 varieties of of trees, shrubs, vines, vegetables, and fruits"—the Fullertons had begun planning for retirement, and the railroad considered closing down the Farm.[120] In 1921, Hal and Edith Fullerton had purchased a twenty-acre plot of land near the railway station in East Setauket for a weekend and holiday retreat and an eventual full-time home. They had named the place "Lorelope," after their three children (Loring, Eleanor, and Hope), and made plans for a series of family-based enterprises at the

East Setauket, Long Island, N. Y.

site. Hal Fullerton even designed a special Lorelope logo and stationery. At first, their daughters and sons-in-law moved into separate cottages on the property. Hope and her husband, Arthur B. (Pat) Tuttle, occupied the house original to the plot; Eleanor and Donald V. Ferguson lived in a newer structure, built by the Fullertons for their retirement. The Tuttles operated a poultry plant and the Fergusons a market garden on the property. Hal and Edith Fullerton also had a canning kitchen constructed. This operation, however, never really developed beyond serving as an outlet or storage place for jams actually prepared by Edith in Medford. In 1925, Eleanor and her husband left Setauket to established an extensive fruit orchard, which they named "Rainbow Ranch," at Middle Island. The Tuttles continued for a short time in charge of the Lorelope Poultry Plant, until Pat became associated with RCA.[121]

At age seventy, after thirty years with the railroad, Hal Fullerton retired from active service, on August 15, 1927. Arrangements had been made and were widely publicized in advance. At the same time, the company announced its intention to abolish the Medford experimental station "because its work of demonstrating the exceptionally great capabilities of Suffolk county's idle lands and the Blessed Isle's extraordinary value in every ramification of agriculture is completed."[122] It also announced the appointment of Edith Fullerton as Director of Agriculture to oversee the final activities of the department.[123] The Fullertons left Medford for East Setauket at the beginning of September.

Plans for disposing of the property quickly could not be realized. A sale was finally authorized in March 1929 and executed nearly a year later, in February 1930. The Farm had continued to function and exhibit produce at the county fairs as late as 1928. After final closing, the railroad agreed to maintain a semblance of the Agricultural Department "for the purpose of supplying information to Long Island producers and those contemplating taking up farming here."[124] Edith Fullerton then devoted most of her time to preparing articles on local farm resources for the railroad's publication office. These pieces, including a handsomely printed pamphlet *Agricultural Long Island* and the lengthy essay, "Long Island Agriculture," which was serialized in the *Long Island Railroad Information Bulletin* and also issued as a separate booklet, featured many of H. B. Fullerton's photographs as illustrations.[125]

Following his official retirement, Hal B. Fullerton engaged in a variety of activities, hobbies, and interests. For a short time, he tried his hand at a commercial nursery business, which used the Lorelope name and address, but was actually based near Yaphank. This venture, developed in partnership with a Japanese-American horticulturalist, "Hunter" Sekine, soon proved unprofitable. Fullerton tabulated and then published his earlier scientific weather observations; "Long Island's Climate: A Five-Year Record Presented by Graphic Chart, 1922–1926," was issued by the Long Island Chamber of Commerce in 1928. He circulated with a series of illustrated lantern-slide talks, especially on horticultural subjects, and often spoke before local garden clubs.[126] When called upon by the press or civic groups, he still spoke and wrote effusively of Long Island's wonderous potential. In 1929, he contributed his baroquely humorous "Meditations of a Long Island Philosopher" to the Home Title Insurance Company's booklet *Ye Long Island Almanack.*

So much of Hal Fullerton's emotional energy and life was enmeshed in his work and calling for the railroad that it was probably inevitable that his retirement and the sale of the Medford Farm would have a serious effect on him. The years of exuberant boostering and boundless enthusiasms could not be maintained forever. Advancing age and a perceived loss of place and purpose exasperated differences and distance between husband and wife. As LIRR Director of Agriculture and now the family's primary breadwinner, Edith became increasingly independent. The rift was palpable and clearly painful to the "senior partner." By 1930, Hal Fullerton's drive was noticeably diminished and he started to become the "rather sad little old man" of his final years.[127]

Edith Fullerton died in Huntington Hospital at age 55, on August 9, 1931, after a period of slow decline. Hal Fullerton lived on for four more years, staying primarily with his daughter and son-in-law, the Fergusons, at Rainbow Ranch, Middle Island. He died of a heart attack in Patchogue Hospital on January 11, 1935.[128]

Epilogue: The Photographs

A journalist associate, Walter S. Funnell, eulogized the late publicist-photographer a year later in a feature article in the *Nassau Daily Review*.[129] Concentrating on Fullerton's accomplishments as the "father of Island road system," Funnell offered a spirited appreciation of his friend's talents and character. Fullerton was "brilliant, far-seeing, enthusiastic, energetic." His "best work," which according to Funnell preceded the experimental farms by several years, was the "hollering" on the subject of good roads. Fullerton made hundreds of public speeches and effectively lobbied and cajoled innumerable boards of supervisors, road overseers, and town officials to realize that good roads enhanced transportation and improved local business. One important key to this success was photography.

"He toted a camera," Funnell wrote, "making pictures eleven-by-fourteen inches, a mechanism as big as a dog house, he often said. He used it with consummate skill. He produced pictures, not mere photographic records." In the end, however,

> the great dog-house camera, the delicate stereopticon, the tanks of oxygen and hydrogen that made possible the brilliant light behind the projector, the day and night journeys, with or without an assistant to aid with the stereopticon—all these are in the discard. Happily a vast number of the photographs remain, as well as the stereopticon slides. One wonders if they may not some day be an important part of the historical record of Long Island, preserved in some suitable museum.

The LIRR Co. Fights Snow by Modern Methods: The Rotary Throws Snow into the Field, Engines with Snow plow near Mineola, November 1898–January 1899 (149.7.1430).

The fate of the photographs remained uncertain for more than a decade. Many years earlier, Hal Fullerton had himself donated a collection of prints of architectural studies of old houses on Long Island to the Metropolitan Museum of Art's Library, Photograph Reference Department. Efforts by family members to interest other organizations in the bulk of the material met with only limited success.[130] During the 1930s, groups of prints, negatives, slides, and publications were dispersed to the United Spanish-American War Veterans (Manhattan Camp No. 1), the State Institute of Applied Agriculture on Long Island (Farmingdale), and the American Museum of Natural History. In the mid-1940s, a large assemblage of the heavy glassplate negatives and other material was salvaged from beneath the porch of the small cottage (the former Canning Kitchen) at the "Lorelope" property in Setauket by its new owner, interested neighbors, and friends and relatives of the photographer. Through a series of fortunate circumstances, the discovery was brought to the attention of officials at the Suffolk County Historical Society in Riverhead, where in 1949, a major share of the items was eventually deposited.

Despite the problems presented by the mass, weight, and deteriorating physical condition of many of the images, the Society recognized the value of the collection and made the commitment to document and preserve it. Over the years, substantial resources have been devoted toward cataloguing, research and identification, proper storage, printing, duplication, and conservation treatment.

The Suffolk County Historical Society's Fullerton Collection has become well known today as an exceptional historic visual source of a

Narcissus poeticus, floral study, c. 1900. Courtesy, Ferguson Collection.

broad range of sights, scenes, events, and activities on Long Island at the turn of the twentieth century. The images, however, emit complex, multiple resonances. On the most rudimentary level they serve as optical documents of aspects of Long Island's past. They are also directed, favored expressions of an idealized view of that past, and case evidence in Fullerton's calls for action—for modernization, change, and improvement, in addition to preservation.

Although Fullerton took obvious pride in his camera work and darkroom technique, he clearly never considered himself either primarily or exclusively a photographer. He came closest to defining his own particular combination of talents and expertise when in 1905 he proclaimed himself a "designer, illustrator, advertising agent."[131] It would probably have been equally appropriate for him to have added: anthologist and picture editor. He seemed less concerned with the creation of individual negatives or prints than in the selection, use, arrangement, placement, and sequencing of multiple images and the interrelation of pictures, text, and graphic devices to inform, amuse, and convince. He was at times as much a compiler, collector, and impresario of others' work as a producer of his own. He seemed equally concerned with the display methods, exhibitry, and performance context of the pictures as the images themselves.

Thus, the collection represents both more and less than Fullerton's own photographic work. Of the approximately 2,200 glassplate negatives, 200 glass-based positives, and 120 film negatives associated with Fullerton at the Suffolk County Historical Society, at least 200 of the glass items—including the earliest dated images—were made by other hands. The work of a number of friends, family members, commercial vendors, and amateur club associates (most notably, Brooklyn Academy of Photography colleague A. R. Pardington) are represented in the collection.

The surviving evidence of Fullerton's own numbering system for his negatives indicates that the Suffolk County Historical Society's collection contains less than one-third of the photographer's work. There are only 503 of the earlier 1,428 registered eleven-by-fourteen-inch plates and approximately 1,670 of almost 7,000 negatives in five-by-seven-inch, five-by-eight-inch, and smaller formats among the Riverhead holdings. Small groups of vintage Fullerton photographic material can also be found at the Queens Public Library, The Museums at Stony Brook, and in several significant private collections.[132]

Fullerton's approach represents both a continuation of and something of a departure from well-established conventions of railroad-sponsored photography in America. During the 1860s and 1870s, the rapidly developing Western and transcontinental lines hired a number of talented photographers to document land survey and construction and to record the scenic wonders available along new

Old Man Haggerty, portrait, Huntington, c. 1902. A Huntington neighbor of the Fullertons, Haggerty ran a cider mill. Courtesy, Ferguson Collection.

Aunt Hannah's Well, Lake Success, 1901
(149.7.137).

The Central Valley—East of Jamaica (Hollis from Dunton's, from Tank Hill), 1901 (149.7.17).

Island Vegetables—Big Crops of Fine Quality, Potato Digger, Peconic, October 1903 (149.7.298).

routes. Among the wet-plate era masters employed in this fashion were the Civil War battlefield veterans Andrew Joseph Russell (1830–1902) and Alexander Gardner (1821–1882), who worked for the Union Pacific Railroad, and William Henry Jackson (1843–1942), who regularly recorded scenes for the Denver and Rio Grande. Other photographers, such as A. A. Hart, C. R. Savage, Carleton E. Watkins (1829–1916), and Eadweard Muybridge (1830–1904), followed the rail lines as entrepreneurs and picture speculators. From the late-1860s into the mid-1880s, this generation of primarily western field photographers produced extraordinary mammoth-plate landscapes (up to twenty-by-twenty-four inches) as well as much smaller stereo views.[133] By the 1880s, advances in photographic technology had removed many of the rigors and much of the novelty from outdoor field work. The advent of the gelatin dry plate and flexible roll and sheet film eliminated the need for the portable darkroom for chemical preparation and immediate development of negatives. The manufacture of presensitized papers for sunlight, darkroom, and projection printing; the availability of faster plate and film emulsions, improved lenses and shutter mechanisms; and the collateral development of a service industry for photo-finishing (developing and printing) had made picture-making simpler, quicker, cheaper, and vastly more accessible. The growing public appetite for photographic images was whetted further by the widespread adoption of the halftone process by newspapers, periodicals, books, pamphlets, and advertising pieces.

American railways sponsored photographic work in the 1880s and 1890s with renewed intensity, as they began to aggressively promote summer and winter holiday leisure travel, suburban development, and commuter service. Among eastern lines, the Pennsylvania system was especially active. It issued illustrated "suburban home" promotional booklets and "holiday tour" and "pleasure tour" guides for trips between New York and Washington, and to Florida, California, the Blue Mountains, the New Jersey shore, the 1893 Columbia Exposition in Chicago, and many other destinations.[134]

William Herman Rau (1855–1920), a highly skilled, artistic professional photographer from Philadelphia, was employed by both the Pennsylvania and Lehigh Railroads in the 1890s and early 1900s.

Mineola, A Glimpse At The Fair, Trotters at Judging Stand, September 1898 (149.7.1581).

Long Beach—Big Wreck, Fullerton Trip, 1901 (149.7.1672).

Rau, whose manner, methods, and aesthetics bear many resemblances to Fullerton's, excelled in topographical work, urban views, portraiture, and stereo-card production. A member of the Photographic Society of Philadelphia, Rau exhibited at the Pennsylvania Academy of Fine Arts in 1889 and 1898 and undertook major commissions for the Pennsylvania Railroad in 1891 and 1893 and for the Lehigh Valley line beginning in 1895. Working under the auspices of the railroads' Passenger Departments and their advertising staffs, he was provided with specially prepared photographic cars and given an engine and crew at his disposal. Using three complete outfits, including one for eighteen-by-twenty-two-inch over-sized plates and a uniquely designed panoramic camera using eighteen-by-forty-seven-and-one-half-inch films, Rau produced dramatic, often picturesque, deeply focused, unmanipulated, large-format views on the main line along the Susquehanna and in the mountains between Altoona and Pittsburg. He also documented "the industries along the line, also all terminals and freight stations and bridges" from New York to Chicago and Saint Louis. Framed eighteen-by-twenty-two-inch prints from a substantial number of these images were displayed by the railroad at the Columbian Exposition in Chicago. Exhibition prints from his Lehigh Valley series, depicting the "railroad scenery" between New York and Niagara Falls, were shown in cities along the sponsor's route and connections.[135]

Whether the two men were aware of each other's work is not known. They were clearly drawn (or commissioned) to photograph many similar subjects. Rau was a superb technician and a meticulous craftsman and printer in both platinum and albumen. Unlike his Long Island contemporary, though, few, if any, of Rau's vintage negatives have survived.[136]

Italian Railroad Gang, probably Medford, 1907 (149.7.435).

Fullerton's achievements centered less on originality or technical finesse than on versatility, range, and a contagious exuberance of spirit. He sought to capture a wide variety of landscapes, atmospheres, and colors encompassing the rural, industrial, suburban, and recreational possibilities made available by the railroad. Although he may have lacked Rau's professional expertise, perfectionism, and panoramic ambition, Fullerton utilized his eleven-by-fourteen-inch outfit with considerable skill and to noteworthy effect.

Unique Long Island was most likely not the first publication of its kind, but it certainly seized upon a timely concept and marked an important trend. In July 1902, the railway and travel trade journal *The Pointer* could comment: "The literature offered by the transportation lines of the United States, Mexico and Canada is taking the magazine form and in many instances the text, the presswork and illustrations are superior to some of the best periodicals." In addition to singling out *Long Island Illustrated* and *Unique Long Island* as among "the handsomest publications of the season," *The Pointer* praised the photographically illustrated books and pamphlets produced by more than seven other lines.[137]

Conclusion

Fullerton possessed an uncanny ability to assume a public vision, to project his personality on a landscape, and claim the locality as his own. He adopted a prevailing popular aesthetic—naturalistic, picturesque, frequently sentimental—and ambitiously attempted to capture the *entirety* of Long Island at the moment it was forced to define itself against the newly created metropolis of Greater New York City. As a visionary and propagandist, Fullerton stands as a transitional figure, a link between the early cosmopolitan era and the technocratic age of Robert Moses and the tract house subdivision. An advocate of suburbanization, modern utilities, and transportation improvement—even a proponent of the automobile— Fullerton remained a progressive-romantic at heart, convinced that agriculture would always remain a critical feature of Long Island's economic and cultural life. He expressed this view most forcefully to the *Brooklyn Eagle* at the time of his retirement from active service with the railroad:

> He foresees a tremendous residential growth for Long Island,
> with New-York working its way eastward at a rapid gait and the

Sand Dune Beach—Amagansett, with Wreck on Beach, December 1902 (149.7.265).

many villages becoming more and more urban in character. But tilling the soil is still to be the main industry, he asserts. 'God, Providence, or whatever you may call it, put Long Island here to feed New York, and it has got to carry out that purpose,' he told an *Eagle* representative a few days ago in his home at Medford.[138]

For Fullerton, not only could the machine and the garden coexist, but each clearly depended on the other. The new garden of the Blessed Isle was in fact made, recorded, promoted, and sold by mechanical means.

By the late 1920s, the Fullertons' progressive-romantic ideology, photographic style, and largely pastoral image of Long Island seemed outmoded to the railroad management and much of the public at large. The population of Nassau and Suffolk Counties—indeed, all of Long Island—continued to climb steadily. Growth was of course most rapid in the metropolitan district at the western end. In 1929, rail passenger volume reached an all-time high of 118,888,228 (61.7 percent of whom were commuters). Usage dropped substantially, and never fully recovered, with the Great Depression and the opening of cheaper-fared subways in central Queens. Railroad freight traffic and revenues, which also rose gradually through the 1910s and 1920s, were similarly affected by the massive national economic failure and new competition from automotive trucking.[139]

Despite the promising experimental beginnings at the Wading River and Medford stations, the successful establishment of Cornell extension programs and the Farmingdale Agricultural College, and the profitable expansion of Suffolk County truck farming through the 1950s, the projected cultivation of the central pine barrens did not materialize. The "home hamper," Hal Fullerton's prized innovation, also would never be widely adopted on Long Island or elsewhere. For the new generation of publicists, the notion of a substantial "Agricultural Long Island" was rapidly being displaced by "America's Sunrise Land."

Yet as image-makers, Hal and Edith Fullerton's influence will continue to be felt. Together, their words and pictures recall the optimism of that critical moment when Long Island's economic and cultural identity appeared richly mixed, charged with potential, and poised in a delicate balance.

Notes

1. Henry Isham Hazelton, *The Boroughs of Brooklyn and Queens, Counties of Nassau and Suffolk, Long Island, New York 1609–1924* (New York: Lewis Historical Publishing Co., 1925), I: 5–6.

2. Hal B. Fullerton, "Meditations of a Long Island Philosopher," *Ye Long Islande Almanack* (Brooklyn: Home Title Insurance Company), vol. 1, no. 1 (January 1929).

3. Hal B. Fullerton, untitled typescript, probably a draft for "Meditations of a Long Island Philosopher," c.1928–29. In private collection of Eleanor Ferguson (daughter of Hal B. and Edith Loring Fullerton), Williston, VT (hereafter cited as Ferguson Collection).

4. The most complete sources of information remain the two characteristically extravagant autobiographical statements he had published much later in life, in 1905 and 1925, when he was already well-established in his second career on Long Island. See H. B. Fullerton, ed., *Twenty-fifth Anniversary Catalogue of the Class of '79, M.I.T.* (New York: Blanchard Press, 1905) and Hazelton, *Boroughs* IV: 346–47.

5. Hazelton, *Boroughs*, IV: 346.

6. Family tradition and currently available documents provide vague and contradictory suggestions regarding the sequence of critical events during this period of Fullerton's youth. His older daughter, Hope F. T. Zarensky, notes in her "Hal B. Fullerton memories," typescript chronology, October 11, 1988, and related correspondence with the author, June 20 and July 11, 1989, that Frances Cordelia Lyon Fullerton died in Cincinnati in 1871. (Mrs. Zarensky cites a letter recently received from the Church Archivist, Episcopal Diocese of Southern Ohio, confirming the date as June 13, 1871, and adding that Frances Fullerton is buried in the Spring Grove Cemetery, Cincinnati.) Mrs. Zarensky also states that it was his *father's* terminal illness, of "Bright's disease" (from which she maintains he died in 1879), that led to Hal's withdrawal from M.I.T. However, according to her sister, Eleanor Ferguson, *As I Remember It* (privately printed, 1978), pp. 4–5, her father claimed that he left M.I.T. out of responsibility for his younger brother Clarence, because "it was unfair to the Kid." Mrs. Ferguson further relates that William R. Fullerton left Cincinnati for Holyoke in 1878, approximately one year after the death of his first wife and remarriage to Sarah Mehitabel, and that, according to a surviving newspaper clipping obituary, William Fullerton died in 1888.

7. Tales of his student days, his friendship with foreign classmate Takuma Dan (later assassinated in Japan), and especially his chemistry lab experiments were recounted years later to his children. See Zarensky, "Fullerton memories"; Eleanor Ferguson, *As I Remember It,* pp. 8–9.

8. *Twenty-fifth Anniversary Catalogue, M.I.T. '79* (1905); "Official Ballot for Officers, Class of '79 M.I.T., 1916," Ferguson Collection.

9. *Twenty-fifth Anniversary Catalogue*; Hal B. Fullerton (HBF) pencil sketches, Ferguson Collection.

10. *Twenty-fifth Anniversary Catalogue* gives date as 1877; a series of pencil sketches in HBF's hand depicting oil field and boardinghouse scenes (in the Ferguson Collection) are dated between March 26 and August 4, 1878.

11. *Twenty-fifth Anniversary Catalogue* personal sketch gives the year 1878; pencil drawings in the Ferguson Collection of the mill are dated Christmas 1878 through April 1880.

12. Zarensky, "Fullerton memories"; Ferguson, *As I Remember It*, p. 9.

13. Newsclipping, *Springfield* [Mass.] *Republican*, October 1, 1896, courtesy of grand-daughter, Mrs. Anne Nauman.

14. *Twenty-fifth Anniversary Catalogue*; Hazelton *Boroughs*, I:5; HBF-Seeger-Guernsey papers, Ferguson Collection.

15. Comic pencil sketches, dated March 11, 1890, Ferguson Collection.

16. HBF-Seeger-Guernsey papers, Ferguson Collection, see especially correspondence of April 11, 1892, and June 30, 1892, and letter outlining new job description and duties in Mexico, June 30, 1892.

17. See letters, August 17, 1892, and October 12, 1892, from C. L. Seeger and February 28, 1893, from R. H. Vaughan in Ferguson Collection.

18. *Springfield Republican*, October 1, 1896; correspondence, Hope F. T. Zarensky with Thomas M. Costello, President, Springfield Library and Museums Association, February 18, 1986, copy in Suffolk County Historical Society (SCHS); papers, Ferguson Collection.

19. Ferguson, *As I Remember It*, p. 11; *Springfield Republican*, October 1, 1896.

20. She is described by her husband as "a Long Island girl of Saxon, Bohemian Gypsy, Holland Dutch and Welsh ancestry" in Hazelton, *Boroughs*, IV: 346. Other sources that mention her Long Island ancestry include: W. Stewart Wallace, comp., *A Dictionary of North American Authors Deceased Before 1950* (Toronto: Ryerson Press, 1951), p. 161; *Who Was Who in America*, I (1897–1942), p. 432; the commemorative notice "Prominent L.I. Woman Dies," *Brooklyn Times* (August 11, 1931). Further biographical information may be found in Ferguson, *As I Remember It*, pp. 13–23. See also Hope F. T. Zarensky, typescript letter to the Editor, *Suffolk County News, Islip Bulletin*, 22 November 1984, regarding 15 November "Weekend" article on Hal and Edith Fullerton (copy on file, SCHS).

21. The Pratt Institute Alumni Affairs Office confirmed that according to official college records, Edith L. Jones (listed as Mrs. H. B. Fullerton) was a "non-graduate" member of the Kindergarten School Class of 1899; telephone conversation with the author, March 1990.

22. Zarensky, "Fullerton memories."

23. *Lain's Brooklyn Directory, 1895* and *Lain's Elite Directory, 1895,* show both men residing at 842 President Street.

24. See photographs, Ferguson Collection.

25. *Brooklyn Daily Eagle Almanac for 1896*, p. 105.

26. "Whirling Dervishes, The Most Unique Wheeling Club Known," *Brooklyn Citizen*, March 8, 1897, p. 10.

27. "Cycling in Brooklyn," *Brooklyn Life* 13 (March 7, 1896): 314.

28. HBF was *not* a member of the Brooklyn Academy of Photography at the time of its founding, although a number of people with whom he later associated (including Frank La Manna, Dr. John Merritt, and William T. Wintringham) were among its founders, according to W.B. Howard, ed., *The Eagle and Brooklyn* (Brooklyn: Brooklyn Daily Eagle, 1893), pp. 786–87.

29. Frank La Manna, William T. Wintringham, Stark W. Lewis, William Arnold, Dr. John Merritt, and A. R. Pardington were all members of both organizations.

30. Other members of his Mexico City social circle also seem to have been practicing amateurs, so it is difficult to assign precise authorship to many of the photographs from the period, most of which are unsigned, still in the possession

of his descendants. (The majority of these are in the Ferguson and Nauman Collections).

31. "Catalogue," Brooklyn Academy of Photography, "Annual Exhibition," May 1901, Ferguson Collection; newsclipping, unidentified Brooklyn paper, April, 1901, Ferguson Collection.

32. The line is now known as the Long Island Rail Road; its earlier name, with "railroad" as one word, is retained here.

33. Eleanor Ferguson, *As I Remember It*, p. 21; photographs, Ferguson Collection.

34. *Twenty-fifth Anniversary Catalogue*; Eleanor Ferguson, *As I Remember It*, p. 23; Hope F. T. Zarensky, typescript notes, "Places of Residence"; Fullerton Collection, SCHS 149.7.660–62.

35. According to Hope F. T. Zarensky, "Places of Residence," n.d., the move from 645 Carleton Ave., Brooklyn, to Central Ave., Hollis, occurred in 1901; *Twenty-fifth Anniversary Catalogue*; Ferguson, *As I Remember It*, p. 25. Regarding Edith Fullerton's tenure at Pratt Institute, see note 21, above.

36. Newsclipping, "Rebuilding an Old House," *The Brooklyn Times* or *Eagle*, November 8, 1902, Ferguson Collection. The house, located on the south side of Main Street, just one building west of Spring Street, was still standing in 1990.

37. Newsclipping, "Eastern Farming," *American Agriculture*, October 24, [c.1902–03], Ferguson Collection.

38. See photographs in Fullerton Collection, SCHS, negative numbers 147.7.1040–44 and .1523–32; Christopher Vagts, *Huntington at the Turn of the Century* (Huntington: Huntington Historical Society, 1974), n.p.

39. Printed handbill "Protect Your Pocketbook," Ferguson Collection.

40. Ferguson, *As I Remember It*, p. 35.

41. Newsclipping, *Brooklyn Times*, July 3, 1901, Ferguson Collection.

42. *Brooklyn Daily Eagle Almanac, 1895*, p. 118; "Cycling Clubs and Their Spheres of Action," *Outing*, August 1897.

43. "Cycling in Brooklyn," *Brooklyn Life* 13 (March 7, 1896): 314.

44. "Finest of All Cycle Parades," *Brooklyn Daily Eagle*, June 28, 1896, p. 5.

45. See "Good Roads" papers, newsclippings, and ephemera, Ferguson Collection, particularly HBF letters to state and national political leaders, June 1900 in "Compositions" scrapbook; HBF's Good Roads Association of Brooklyn Life Membership card; G.R.A. of Brooklyn Official Ballot of November 16, 1897; invitation and other items relating to the opening of Return Cycle Path, Brooklyn, June 26, 1896; HBF League of American Wheelmen Membership Card, 1901; *Brooklyn Eagle*, March 5, 1897 on Brooklyn Cycle Show; Special Cycle Path Police correspondence, May 5, 1896; and H. B. Fullerton, "Get into Politics and Get There Quick," *The L.A.W. Magazine*, tearsheet, c. 1900–01. Also *Fifty Miles Around New York* (League of American Wheelmen, 1897).

46. *Cyclists' Paradise, Long Island* (Long Island City, N.Y.: Long Island Railroad Co., 1897 [SCHS Collection] and 1898 [Ferguson Collection]).

47. Handbill for "Patent Combination Closed Passenger and Bicycle Car," patented June 9, 1900, Ferguson Collection.

48. Newsclipping, *American Cyclist*, October 27, 1897, Ferguson Collection.

49. Newsclipping, *Long Island Democrat*, November 9, 1897, Ferguson Collection.

50. *Cyclists' Paradise, Long Island*, p. 1.

51. The initial volumes of this publication were unfortunately not dated; close comparison of extant copies in the collections of the Suffolk County Historical Society, New York Public Library, Society for the Preservation of Long Island Antiquities, and The Museums at Stony Brook indicated that the "Occident to Orient" edition (at SCHS) clearly contained the earliest datable photographs—the caption for one of which cites the 1897 annual record for duck farm production (while other volumes refer to the 1898 record). The 1900 and 1901 editions are both clearly dated on the back covers. The 1902 edition, which is completely redesigned, sports a relief map of Long Island and the subtitle "Camera Sketches" on its cover. The most distinctive feature of the 1904 edition, which has a cover and subtitle similar to the 1902 volume, is that the halftones are printed onto a light green colored ground.

52. Newsclipping, *Brooklyn Times,* June 1, 1901, Ferguson Collection.

53. *Unique Long Island,* Camp Black Edition, frontispiece (SCHS).

54. *Unique Long Island,* "Two Great Spanish-American War Camps" Edition, title page; see also *Unique Long Island,* 1900 and 1901 editions.

55. See HBF to W. F. Potter, January 20, 1902, Ferguson Collection.

56. Murphy was a long-term member in Brooklyn's second-oldest cycling organization, the King's County Wheelmen. His name appears as as a record-holder in the club listings in the *Brooklyn Daily Eagle Almanac*; see, for instance, 1892 issue, pp. 65–66; and 1896 issue, p. 104.

57. Newsclipping, "Murphy's Record Mile," *The Cycling Gazette,* n.d. [c.1899], p. 48, Ferguson Collection.

58. Useful sources on Fullerton and Murphy include Ron Ziel and George Foster, *Steel Rails to Sunrise* (New York: Hawthorne Books, 1965), pp. 68–69; Ferguson, "Cycling and Good Roads," in *As I Remember It*; "A Mile in Less Than a Minute on a Bicycle," *Scientific American,* July 15, 1899, pp. 41–42; H. B. Fullerton, mimeographed typescript letter to "Cycling Editors," June 22, 1899; clipping, *Harper's Weekly,* n.d., 1899; clipping, "A Wonderful Feat," *New York Sun,* June 22, 1899; clipping, "Murphy's Marvelous Ride," *The Cycling West,* n.d., [c.July], 1899; clipping, "Murphy's Record Mile," *The Cycling Gazette,* [c. 1899]; Charles M. Murphy, "Laughed at Murphy Who Said He Could Ride Behind Fastest Engine on the L.I. Railroad," (four-part series), *Queens County Evening News* (1929), reprinted as Charles M. Murphy, *A Mile-A-Minute-Career,* in *A Story of the Railroad and a Bicycle* (Jamaica, NY: Jamaica Law Printing, n.d. [c.1929]); clipping, "Murphy's Great Ride," *The Springfield Sunday Union,* November 4, 1900; clipping, "Rides Mile in 57–4/5 Seconds," *Worcester Sunday Telegram,* October 28, 1900; these and other clippings on the ride are in the Ferguson Collection.

The suggestion that Murphy's ride was intended as a "scientific experiment in streamlining" is made by Ethel Booth Urbahn in "The Adventurous Booths," *Long Island Forum* 37 (October 1974): 197 and in the title page inscription of Murphy's obviously retrospective *A Mile-A-Minute Career*. Among contemporary commentators, however, only the *Scientific American* seems to have recognized these implications, when it concluded (p. 42): "Without disparaging in any degree the persistence and pluck of the bicyclist, the most interesting feature of the ride is the impressive object lesson it affords as to the serious nature of atmospheric resistance on moving bodies."

The first modern scientific studies in the field of aerodynamics were in fact being conducted at precisely this time—by aviation researchers. It is worth noting that the Wright brothers, whose interests and mechanical skills derived, coincidentally, to a large extent from their bicycle shop operating experience, were among the pioneers in the field. Several early attempts at locomotive contouring were made in Germany in 1904 and 1912. Only after the First World War, however, was the discipline more widely applied to the study and construction of land vehicle forms, particularly automobiles, railroad cars and engines. "Streamlining" did not truly come into vogue as a popular design principle for machinery, decoration, and consumer goods in the United States until the late-1920s and 1930s. See, for instance, Siegfried Giedeon's classic study, *Mechanization Takes Command* (New York: W. W. Norton, 1969), pp. 607–11; John R. Stilgoe, *Metropolitan Corridor: Railroads and the American Scene* (New Haven: Yale University Press, 1983), pp. 57–59; and the recent article by James J. Flink, "The Path of Least Resistance," *American Heritage of Invention & Technology,* 5:2 (Fall 1989): 34–44.

59. Newsclipping, *Brooklyn Times,* December 19, 1900. Fullerton's friend (and fellow cyclist-photographer) A. R. Pardington was also an officer in the auto club. On the early automobile age on Long Island, see Robert Miller, "The Long Island Motor Parkway: Prelude to Robert Moses," in Joann P. Krieg, ed., *Robert Moses: Single-Minded Genius* (Interlaken, NY: Heart of the Lakes, 1989), pp. 151–67.

60. *Collier's Weekly,* 27:5 (May 4, 1901): 24–25.

61. Typescript memorandum, WHB to HBF, April 26, 1901, Ferguson Collection; see also newsclipping, *Brooklyn Daily Eagle,* April 20, 1901, Ferguson Collection.

62. Useful sources on this incident include the following items in the Ferguson Collection: Newsclipping, "Automobile Smashed by L.I.R.R. Engine," *Brooklyn Daily Times,* October 30, 1901; H. B. Fullerton, typescript memoranda to W. F. Potter, L.I.R.R. General Superintendent, "Details Covering Automobile Accident—Westbury, L.I., Wednesday, October 30, 1901," and correspondence dated Nov. 21, 1901 and Jan. 20, 1902; clipping, "Fullerton Rejoices," *Suffolk Bulletin,* October 31, 1902.

63. See, especially, newsclippings in Ferguson Collection: "How to Boom a Horse Show," *Brooklyn Daily Times,* August 17, 1901; "Bay Shore's First Horse Show Has a Most Brilliant Opening," *New York Herald,* August 10, 1901; "Bay Shore Horse Show Ends in Blaze of Glory," *Brooklyn Daily Eagle,* August 11, 1901.

64. As described in *Long Island Railroad Men* 2:6 (April 1899) and 6:3 (March 1903).

65. Broadside for Lecture, East Quogue, February 1, 1901; Invitation card for illustrated lecture, American Institute, April 2, 1901, Ferguson Collection.

66. See, for instance, "Some Notable Amateur Photographs of the Year," *The Commercial Advertiser,* January 6, 1900; "Duck Shooting," *The Commercial Advertiser,* September 20, 1900; "Scenes Along the Shore of Long Island," *The Commercial Advertiser,* June 13, 1903; "Scenes along the Route" [of the LIRR], *Brooklyn Times,* April 21, 1900; "A Remarkable Cedar Tree A Natural Ornament at Huntington Harbor," *Brooklyn Times,* March 16, 1901; "Beautiful Lloyd's Harbor," *Brooklyn Times,* March 23, 1901; "The New State Park at Southampton," *Brooklyn Times,* November 29, 1902; article on LIRR snow removal, *Brooklyn Times,* February 28, 1903; article with photographs of "Edward Thompson and Smithtown's Biggest Trout," "A Huntington Beauty Spot," and "Old Willow Tree at Smithtown." *Brooklyn Times,* May 23, 1903; "At Amagansett," *New York Press,* July 12, 1901; "Long Island," *The World,* May 10, 1903; "Long Island to Profit By Brooklyn's Overflow," *The World,* June 19, 1904; *New York Herald's* Brooklyn Supplement on Huntington's 250th Anniversary Celebration, July 1903; "The Captain Investigates," *The Photo-American,* July 1901; "'Long Shore on Long Island," *New York*

Daily Tribune, August 25, 1901; and *Long Island Breeze* magazine, September 1901.

67. See also, "Long Island: Its Summer Resorts, Seaside and Suburban—Fine Roads for Horses and Carriages, Automobiles and Bicycles," *The Hub,* July 1901; "Long Island, Beauty Spots on the Shores of the Elongated Piece of Land Surrounded by Water," *The Buffalo Illustrated Times,* June 29, 1902; "Bridgehampton Windmill," *The American Miller,* May 1, 1902; "Old Grist Mill at Hempstead, Long Island," *American Hay, Flour and Feed Journal,* October 1902; "Long Island in Summer" and "Summer Travel Literature," *The Pointer,* July 1902; "Long Island's Historic Houses," *Boston Home Journal: An Illustrated Paper of Society and Travel,* September 19, 1903; "Long Island," *The Amateur Sportsman and Sportsman's Magazine,* c. August 1901; "Long Island Attractions," *The Summer Travel Guide,* June 8, 1901.

68. Correspondence, F. N. Doubleday to H. B. Fullerton, August 21, 1902 and W. H. Baldwin to H. B. Fullerton, September 18, 1901 (enclosing Walter H. Page to W. H. Baldwin, September 4, 1901), Ferguson Collection; see also Associated Press clipping, "F. N. Doubleday, Publisher, 72 Dies in Florida," January 30, 1934, "Compositions" scrapbook, Ferguson Collection.

69. H. B. Fullerton, "Abundio's Aztec Turkey," *Pittsburg Leader,* December 12, 1902. When turkey is not available, iguana is prepared as a substitute.

70. On the title page of the copy of *How to Make a Flower Garden: A Manual of Practical Information and Suggestions,* in the Suffolk County Historical Society Library, the publication date is printed as 1905; the copyright page, however, is inscribed "Copyright, 1901, 1902, 1903, by Doubleday, Page & Company Published, November, 1903." The volume contains the articles "Annual Vines to Conceal Rubbish" by "The Fullertons" (pp. 106–7) and "The Home Window Garden" by "Edith Loring Fullerton" (pp. 175–88). Photographs credited to Hal Fullerton appear on pp. 106, 179, and 180.

71. "How to Make a Vegetable Garden," *Brooklyn Citizen,* May 7, 1905; "A New Outdoor Book For Nature Lovers," *Brooklyn Eagle,* April 22, 1905.

72. Edith Loring Fullerton, *How to Make a Vegetable Garden: A Practical and Suggestive Manual for the Home Garden* (New York: Doubleday, Page & Company, 1905), pp. vii and 335.

73. *Properties of the Matawok Land Company—Newtown, Jamaica, Rocky Point, Bridgehampton* (New York, Blanchard Press, n.d. [c.1905]), Ferguson Collection. The frontispiece of this intriguing pamphlet notes that the company, represented by Smith & Stewart, 45 William and 43 Pine Streets, New York City, was "incorporated under the laws of the state of New York, February, 1903." The booklet includes a trial balance financial statement dated "February 2nd, 1905." William F. Potter is listed as one of the directors.

74. Felix E. Reifschneider, "History of the Long Island Railroad," in *LIRR Information Bulletin,* 3:4 (September 30, 1924): 13–15; also "Long Island Railroad" in Hazelton, *Boroughs* I:384–420. After William Baldwin's death, William F. Potter succeeded briefly to the presidency of the LIRR in January 1905. Potter died suddenly and was followed by Ralph Peters in April 1905.

75. As part of its effort to increase freight traffic during the nineteenth century, the railroad had commissioned a study of the agricultural possibilities of the undeveloped "wild lands" in the center of Suffolk County. Though the LIRR even published the report of this investigation, *The Wild Lands of Long Island* (1860), the recommendation that a program be established to demonstrate "proof by actual cultivation" was virtually ignored until 1905, a decade after the line's North

Shore Branch was extended to Wading River. See Edith Loring Fullerton, "Long Island Agriculture," Chap. 3, *LIRR Information Bulletin*, 6:4 (October-November 1929): 21–24. This work was also issued in slightly abbreviated form as a separate booklet: Edith Loring Fullerton, *History of Long Island Agriculture* (n.p. [New York]: Long Island Railroad, n.d [c.1930]), pp. 12–14.

76. "Waste Land in Long Island Made Into Good Farms: Practical Method Adopted by the Railroad Company to Develop Its Territory," *Craftsman*, 18 (August 1910): 582–85.

77. The American Railway Development Association "Proceedings of a Special Meeting of the Executive Committee, Chicago, Illinois, October 19, 1942" includes, on pp. 109–10, brief "Historical Notes" on the origin of the organization and accounts of its earliest meetings, its Constitution, and various name changes. The group was established in Chicago, October 17, 1906, as the American Railway Industrial Association. It held its first annual meeting in the same city on January 8, 1907. The organization was known as the Railway Industrial Association (1911), the Railway Development Association (1913), and finally the American Railway Development Association (1920). The A.R.D.A.'s "Constitution" and a list of members can be found in the "Proceedings of the Nineteenth Annual Meeting, Hotel Statler, Detroit, Michigan, June 8–10, 1927." The "Proceedings of the Annual Meeting, St. Paul Hotel, St. Paul, Minnesota, May 11–13, 1915" includes (on pp. 53–54) a toast to and short speech by Edith Fullerton, then officially Assistant Director, Agricultural Development, LIRR.

78. In 1907, for instance, the Fullertons arranged to visit the Pennsylvania Railroad's experimental farm in Wooster, Ohio, which was under the direction of Charles E. Thorne, according to correspondence, Office of the President, Pennsylvania Railroad, to Mrs. H. B. Fullerton, October 22, 1907, Ferguson Collection. Also, at least by 1911, the Pennsylvania was operating still another model farm on the Delmarva Penninsula (as indicated in the *Long Island Agronomist*, September 1, 1911 issue). Ferguson, *As I Remember It*, notes that the Norfolk and Western operated an experimental farm, which raised goats, around 1908 in West Virginia (p. 36).

79. Edith Loring Fullerton, *The Lure of the Land, The History of a Market-Garden and Dairy Plot Developed within Eight Months upon Long Island's Idle Territory, Long Designated as "Scrub Oak Waste," and "Pine Barrens,"* 4th ed. (Long Island: Long Island Railroad Company, 1912), p. 9. The site of the Wading River Farm was later purchased by the Long Island Lighting Company (LILCO) and became part of the roadway entrance to the Shoreham Nuclear Power Plant, as noted by Chester M. Chorzempa in "A Developmental History of the Hamlet of Wading River and the Influence of the Long Island Railroad Experimental Farm No. 1," graduate course paper, SUNY Stony Brook, April 5, 1979, copy on file SCHS, p. 32. Edited portions of this study were subsequently published as Chet Chorzempa, "The LIRR and Peace and Plenty Farm at Wading River," *Long Island Forum* 43 (Dec. 1980): 254–58, which was then supplemented by Chet Chorzempa and F. R. DePetris, "The LIRR and Its Experimental Farms, Part II, A Photographic Essay," *Long Island Forum* 45 (April 1982): 71–74. A second graduate paper by the same author treats the story of the Wading River farm from a somewhat different perspective and adds suggestive new economic data and analysis: see Chester M. Chorzempa, "The Long Island Railroad and The Experimental Farms at Wading River—An Economic Overview," (1980), on file, SCHS.

80. E. Fullerton, *Lure*, p. 12; Fullerton Collection photographs, SCHS, numbers 149.7.507 & .732–.735; Salvatore J. LaGumina, "Fullerton and The

Italians: Experiment in Agriculture," *Long Island Forum,* 52:1 (Winter 1989): 12–20.

81. E. Fullerton, *Lure,* p. 10.

82. See ibid., p. 12, and Chorzempa, "The Long Island Railroad and The Experimental Farms at Wading River" (1980), p. 13. See also Chorzempa, "The LIRR and Peace and Plenty Farm at Wading River," *Long Island Forum* 43 (Dec. 1980): 256.

83. E. Fullerton, *Lure,* p. 18; "Long Island Agriculture," *LIRR Information Bulletin* 6:4 (Oct.-Nov. 1929): 16.

84. E. Fullerton, *Lure,* p. 71.

85. *Riverhead News,* September 22, 1906, p. 2.

86. *Long Island Agronomist,* "Farewell Issue" 8:4 (November 1, 1914), quoted in Ferguson, *As I Remember It,* p. 111.

87. *Long Island Agronomist* 8:4, quoted in Ferguson, *As I Remember It,* p. 111.

88. See Hope F. T. Zarensky, "Places of Residence"; E. Fullerton, *Lure,* p. 84; Ferguson, *As I Remember It,* pp. 35–36.

89. E. Fullerton, *Lure,* pp. 86–88.

90. Ferguson, *As I Remember It,* pp. 49–51.

91. See ibid., pp. 129–30, on the class divisions among the farm managers, staff, and families and the laborers and local farmers and tradesmen.

92. Ida Medeck, "Medford Through the Years," in *1776–1976 Medford, Long Island, New York, Bicentennial Celebration* (Medford: Medford Bicentennial Committee, 1976), pp. 13–15.

93. See H. B. Fullerton's Progressive Party membership certificate, Ferguson Collection.

94. Theodore Roosevelt's visit is described in Ferguson, *As I Remember It,* pp. 68–71, and documented in Fullerton Collection photographs, SCHS, negative number 147.7.1705.

95. Newsclipping, "Patchogue Filled with Suffragists . . . Mrs. Fullerton a Speaker," *Brooklyn Eagle,* May 30, 1914, Ferguson Collection.

96. E. Fullerton, *Lure,* pp. 91–93; "Mrs. Fullerton on Long Island Truck Farming," *The Brooklyn Standard Union,* April 24, 1910; Edith Loring Fullerton, "Long Island Agriculture," Chap. 4, *LIRR Information Bulletin* 6:5 (Jan.-Feb. 1930): 21; *Long Island Agronomist* 8:4 (November 1, 1914), quoted in Ferguson, *As I Remember It,* p. 111.

97. *The Brooklyn Standard Union,* April 24, 1910; E. Fullerton, *Lure,* p. 89.

98. Edith Loring Fullerton, "Long Island Agriculture," *LIRR Information Bulletin* 6:5 (Jan.-Feb. 1930): 22–24; also Chap. 5, in *LIRR Information Bulletin* 6:6 (March-April-May 1930): 52–53.

99. Edith Loring Fullerton, *Small Gardens for Small Folks* (Philadelphia: W. Atlee Burpee & Co., 1912). See also "Family Nicknames," Ferguson, *As I Remember It,* n.p.

100. Edith Loring Fullerton, *The Book of the Home Garden* (New York and London: D. Appleton and Company, 1919). The 260-page work is similar to the successful 1905 *How to Make a Vegetable Garden* in format, approach, and style, but is written explicitly for a younger audience. The later volume is also less finely designed and printed, and contains fewer illustrations, which depict the family and garden at Medford (rather than Huntington).

101. Edith Loring Fullerton, "Long Island Agriculture," *LIRR Information Bulletin* 6:5 (Jan.-Feb. 1930): 22–23; Ferguson, *As I Remember It,* p. 127. See also, for

instance, "Supplement" to *Long Island Agronomist* 7:8 (March 1, 1914), "Long Island Young Folks' Corn, Potato and Cauliflower Clubs," in Ferguson Collection.

102. Edith L. Fullerton, "Long Island Agriculture," in *LIRR Information Bulletin* 6:5 (Jan.-Feb. 1930): 24. The medal is preserved in the SCHS collection (see SCHS artifact inventory numbers I 4391–4392). Another award medal is used as an illustratation in Chap. 3 of "Long Island Agriculture," in *LIRR Information Bulletin* 6:4 (Oct.-Nov. 1929): 25.

103. Advertising pamphlet, *What the Fullertons did with Scrub Cows* (Detroit: The Larrowe Milling Co., 1913), Ferguson Collection; Ferguson, *As I Remember It*, pp. 53–55 and 84–85.

104. *Long Island Agronomist* 7:9 (April 1, 1914): 3.

105. *Long Island Agronomist* 8:4 quoted in Ferguson, *As I Remember It*, pp. 111–12.

106. *Long Island Agronomist* 7:9 (April 1, 1914): 10–16, includes *The Long Island Tryst* 1:1 (March 1914), produced by W. P. Hartman, Chief of the Bureau.

107. Felix E. Reifschneider, "History of the Long Island Railroad," *LIRR Information Bulletin* 3:6 (March 16, 1925): 57–58.

108. There were four other committee members, Clyde Lyndon King (Chairman, University of Pennsylvania), Arthur J. Anderson (editor, *Pennsylvania Farmer*), Cyrus C. Miller (former Bronx Borough President), and Paul Work (Cornell University). The report, dated November 19, 1914, was published by the National Municipal League, Philadelphia, in 1915. The work of the committee, which sought to improve efficiency and lower the cost of the urban food supply, was supported by Samuel S. Fels of Philadelphia and Charles J. Brand, Chief of the National Bureau of Markets. The report concentrated on the effort to eliminate "all four types of middlemen [involved in the urban marketing and distribution of agricultural produce]—the country buyer, the wholesale receiver, the jobber, and the retailer." Fullerton, who was praised as having "practically nationalized the use of the hamper as a means of direct shipment," discussed the need for state support of farmers' cooperative organizations and the active involvement of these associations in the creation of better urban marketing facilities and new strategies to manage mail, express, and telephone orders, grading, packing, and continuous shipping (pp. 25–26). "In the near future," he remarked, "Long Island potatoes, asparagus, oysters, cauliflower, apples, can be promptly obtained by phone, by letter or by personal solicitation at regularly established offices or depots in our great cities. Eastern shore sweet potatoes, Cape Cod cranberries, or late grapes will be obtained in exactly the same way at a far lower charge to the producer than under the present plan."

109. "Women Will Tackle Living Cost Problem," *Philadelphia Record* (September 27, 1914), includes a halftone portrait of Edith Fullerton. The article describes the conference scheduled by representatives of the principal women's social and economic organizations of Philadelphia. The meeting was called by leaders of the Vegetable Growers' Association to explore ways of combatting the high cost of living and to "learn the causes of the present advanced cost of edibles and the differences in the prices the farmer receives for his product and the price the ultimate consumer—the householder—has to pay for the same products."

110. On the Long Island Railroad during World War I, see Felix E. Reifschneider, "History of the Long Island Railroad," *LIRR Information Bulletin* 3:6 (March 16, 1925): 56–68; also Ziel and Foster, *Steel Rails*, pp. 162–63.

111. Reifschneider, "History of LIRR," p. 57.

112. Ibid., p. 58; also *Long Island Food Reserve Battalion Food Preservation Instruction Train* [pamphlet] (May 1917), Ferguson Collection.

113. Ferguson, *As I Remember It*, pp. 164–66; E. Fullerton, *The Book of the Home Garden*, pp. vii-viii.

114. Ferguson, *As I Remember It*, pp. 183–201; James H. Collins, "Farming the Shell Craters of France," *The Country Gentleman* (November 6, 1920), pp. 10ff; A.H. Folwell, "Texts From the Gospel of Get-There-First: A Man Who Couldn't, But Did," *Leslie's Weekly* (September 11, 1920); and newsclipping, "Fullerton in France," *Southampton Star*, June 25, 1920, which quotes from H. B. Fullerton's correspondence with LIRR president Ralph Peters about the trip.

115. Quoted in Collins, "Farming the Shell Craters," p. 10.

116. See especially Collins, "Farming the Shell Craters," and Folwell, "Texts From the Gospel of Get-There-First," cited in note 114 above.

117. *Long Island Agronomist* 6:8, as cited in Ferguson, *As I Remember It*, pp. 125–26.

118. "Long Island Can Produce Sugar Beets That Outrank Country's Best at Utah; Could Meet All New York City's Needs," *Brooklyn Daily Eagle*, September 26, 1920. See also: photographs and "Railroad's Demonstration Farm Exhibit Wins Fresh Laurels at Riverhead Fair," in *LIRR Information Bulletin* 2:7 (December 3, 1923): 10; "Sugar Beet Growers On Long Island Increase Over 100% in Number Last Year" and "Establishment of Sugar Beet Factory on Long Island Awaits Favorable Decision on Tariff Question," in *LIRR Information Bulletin* 3:6 (March 16, 1925): 62–64; Hazelton, *Boroughs* IV: 404–12; and "Long Island Sugar Beets, 1920" photograph album, The Museums at Stony Brook Collection.

119. Edith Fullerton outlined her design for a "model kitchen" in "Take Thought for Kitchen Comfort," *American Agriculturist* (May 31, 1924), and "Mrs. Fullerton's Model Long Island Kitchen," *LIRR Information Bulletin* (September 30, 1924). Both articles contain illustrations from photographs of the interior of the Medford Homestead. On Edith Fullerton's official appointment as Assistant Director of Agriculture, see note 77, above.

120. "Experimental Farm Is Sold to Private Party by Railroad," *Patchogue Advance*, February 11, 1930.

121. "Lorelope," *LIRR Information Bulletin* 3:6 (March 16, 1925): 28–29. According to Eleanor Ferguson (personal correspondence with the author, April 8, 1989), this article contains many inaccuracies; these have been corrected in the present text in response to her suggestions. Loring Fullerton (1908–1973) spent most of the 1920s at school, living away from Long Island—at the Storm King School (Cornwall-on-Hudson), Swavely (Virginia), and Michigan State University, where he studied forestry and landscape design. He later worked at a number of nurseries and attempted several such enterprises of his own, at first on Long Island and then New Jersey. He lived with the Fergusons at Rainbow Ranch, Middle Island during the 1930s. For an account of his life, including his unfortunate experiences in the navy during World War II, see Ferguson, *As I Remember It*, pp. 251–58.

122. Hal Fullerton's retirement was widely reported in the New York regional press. Many celebratory articles appeared, including: Frank P. Johnson, "Performed Agricultural Miracle," *Brooklyn Eagle*, August 14, 1927, p. 13; [Huntington] *Long Islander*, August 19, 1927; [Sayville] *Suffolk County News*, August 19, 1927; *Patchogue Advance*, September 7, 1927. See also correspondence relating to HBF retirement, Ferguson Collection. On the planned and actual sale and disposal of the Medford Farm see correspondence, Ferguson Collection;

"From Hal Fullerton," *Valley Stream Record,* August 19, 1927; "To Abolish Model Farm," *New York Times,* August 25,1927; and *Patchogue Advance,* February 11, 1930.

123. On Edith Fullerton's appointment see Marion Clyde McCarroll, "Once a Pioneer Farmer on Long Island, She Now Becomes a Railroad Official," *New York Evening Post,* January 27, 1928, and correspondence, Ferguson Collection.

124. "Experimental Farm Is Sold to Private Party by Railroad," *Patchogue Advance,* February 11, 1930.

125. *Agricultural Long Island* (New York: Agriculture Department of the Long Island Railroad Co., n.d. [c.1928–29]), 16 pp., Ferguson Collection; *LIRR Information Bulletin* 6:2 through 6:6 (April-May 1929 through March-April-May 1930). See also note 75, above.

126. The Lorelope Nursery project is described in "Raising Rare Plants of Japan in Nursery at West Yaphank," *Patchogue Advance,* May 11, 1928. An exuberant account of Hal and Edith Fullerton's relationship and their anniversary flight on a Fairchild cabin monoplane appears in "Age No Barrier for Flyers, say Fullertons, Wed 30 Years," *Brooklyn Daily Times,* October 7, 1928. Hal Fullerton advertised "Three 1 Hour Picture Talks" with "Lantern slides, many in color" ("Worthwhile Vegetables and Shrubs," "Flowers and Shrubs for the Home," and "Joys of Country Children") in *Horticulture* magazine (October 1, 1928). He addressed the Mayflower Chapter, Setauket D.A.R. on "Spring Gardens" in April 1930 (according to the *Port Jefferson Times,* May 1, 1930).

127. Eleanor Ferguson gives a poignant account of her parents' differences at the end of their lives and her father's decline in *As I Remember It* (pp. 1 and 271–74).

128. Obituaries for Edith Fullerton appeared in many papers, including the *Brooklyn Times,* August 11, 1931, in which her death is attributed to a heart attack. She had had a hysterectomy three months before, and had never fully recovered from the operation. See, also, Ferguson, *As I Remember It,* p. 273, and Riverhead, Suffolk County Surrogate Office, File 322 P (1931). Notices of H. B. Fullerton's passing were published in the *Patchogue Advance, Brooklyn Eagle,* and *New York Herald Tribune,* January 13, 1935; *New York Times,* January 12, 1935, p. 15; [Huntington] *Long Islander,* January 18, 1935.

129. "Hal Fullerton—Long Island Road Builder," *Nassau Daily Review,* March 3, 1936.

130. Hope Fullerton Tuttle Zarensky, correspondence and notes, "Where Various of Dad's collections were sent," in "Compositions" scrapbook, Ferguson Collection. See, especially, letters from Alice L. Felton, Photograph Division, Library, Metropolitan Museum of Art (June 5 and July 8, 1937); H. B. Knapp, Director, State Institute of Applied Agriculture on Long Island (November 30, 1934 and August 23, 1937); Major Bernard A. Reinold, Perry Williams Home, East Islip, NY (January 25, 1935); and R. D. W. Ewing and William Whiting of the Whiting Paper Company, Holyoke, Massachusetts (April 5 and 23, 1949).

131. Imprinted on the covers of two booklets, *Properties of the Matawok Land Company—Newtown, Jamaica, Rocky Point, Bridgehampton* and *Twenty-fifth Anniversary Catalogue of the Class of '79, M.I.T.*

132. There are sixty-seven lantern slides (including two autochromes) and the original album of five-by-seven-inch prints entitled "Long Island Sugar Beets, 1920" at The Museums at Stony Brook. The Long Island Division of the Queensborough Public Library in Jamaica retains twenty-six five-by-seven-inch glass negatives (Fullerton's original numbers 4371 through 4397), mostly views of

officials and events associated with the American and Long Island Automobile Clubs, 1901 and 1904, which were obtained from Samuel B. Cross. One of the most significant private holdings of vintage Fullerton images, part of the Ron Ziel Collection, Water Mill, New York, was acquired in 1989–1990 by the Queensborough Public Library. When I visited Mr. Ziel to survey his collection in September 1988, it contained approximately 105 of Fullerton's five-by-seven-inch negatives and one partial eleven-by-fourteen-inch plate, relating primarily to railroad operations (most of which are reproduced in Ziel and Foster's *Steel Rails to Sunrise*). Several of the photographer's descendants, most notably his daughter Eleanor Ferguson and granddaughter Anne F. Nauman, possess important groups of prints, lantern slides, and documents. It is likely that additional vintage Fullerton prints and plates exist in other local museums, historical societies, and private collections. The Suffolk County Historical Society's collection, however, clearly remains the preeminent body of surviving work—probably encompassing less than one third of H. B. Fullerton's lifetime production.

133. See Weston J. Neff and James N. Wood, *Era of Exploration: The Rise Of Landscape Photography in the American West, 1860–1885* (Boston: Albright-Knox Gallery and the Metropolitan Museum of Art, 1975), pp. 42–49. Also Beaumont Newhall, *The History of Photography from 1839 to Present,* rev. ed. (New York: The Museum of Modern Art, 1982), pp. 94–103.

134. At least a dozen of the Pennsylvania Railroad Company's "holiday tour" booklets can be found in the New York Public Library's research library collection. The cultural geography created by the American railroad industry between 1880 and 1930—and the photography and artwork both funded and inspired by the railroads during this period (including Rau's)—are expertly treated in John Stilgoe, *Metropolitan Corridor,* particularly pp. 158–61.

135. See Rau's two extremely informative personal accounts: "Railroad Photography," in the *American Journal of Photography* (April 1897): 169–75; and "How I Photograph Railway Scenery," *Photo Era* 36:6 (June 1916). Other useful sources on Rau include: William Brey, "On the Rails with William Rau," *Photographica* 17:2 (September 1988): 3–5; Kenneth Finkel, *Nineteenth-century Photography in Philadelphia* (New York: Dover and The Library Company of Philadelphia, 1980), pp. 3, 20, 49, 142, 154, 165–69, 201, 216, and 218; Edward Pare and Phyllis Lambert, *Photography and Architecture, 1839–1959* (Montreal: Canadian Centre for Architecture, 1982), p. 257 and plates 107–8; and Sarah Greenough et al., *On the Art of Fixing a Shadow: One Hundred and Fifty Years of Photography* (Washington, DC: National Gallery of Art and the Art Institute of Chicago, 1989), pp. 477, 492, and plate 108. Not only did Rau seek out railroad and landscape scenes, but, as Finkel shows, he also took pictures of Theodore Roosevelt giving speeches, and made autochrome still-lifes of produce, fruits and vegetables.

136. Approximately 600 high-quality vintage prints of Rau's railroad views are presently known to survive in museum, library, and private collections. I am indebted to Ken Finkel, Library Company of Philadelphia, and Sarah McNear, Allentown Art Museum, for providing information and suggesting sources on Rau.

137. "Summer Travel Literature," *The Pointer,* July 1902, also singles out the publications of the Missouri Pacific; Boston & Maine; Bangor & Aroostock; Chicago, Rock Island & Pacific; Pere Marquette; and the Wabash railways.

138. Frank P. Johnson, "Performed Agricultural Miracle," *Brooklyn Eagle,* August 14, 1927.

139. Passenger volume is discussed by Ziel and Foster in *Steel Rails*, p. 121. Population figures are summarized in Long Island Regional Planning Board, *Historical Population of Long Island Communities 1790–1980: Decennial Census Data*, (Hauppauge, NY: Long Island Regional Planning Board, August 1982). On the volume of and revenue from railroad freight traffic, see: Chester M. Chorzempa, "The Long Island Railroad and The Experimental Farm at Wading River—An Economic Overview," (SCHS), pp. 19–23.

About the Author

Charles L. Sachs is a specialist in historical photography and the material culture of the greater New York metropolitan region. A native Long Islander, he is the author of *A Casual Witness: Photographs from the Hawkins Family Collection* (1978) and *Made on Staten Island: Agriculture, Industry, and Suburban Living in the City* (1988). He is currently Curator and Director of the Permanent Exhibition at the South Street Seaport Museum in New York City.

Index

Numbers in **bold** refer to photographs

The Suffolk County Historical Society

The Suffolk County Historical Society, founded in 1886, is the oldest historical society in Suffolk and Nassau Counties. Its purposes include the collection, preservation, and interpretation of objects and printed materials relating to Suffolk County and its people. The permanent and changing exhibition program in the Society's museum highlights important themes in Suffolk County history through the study of material culture. Its library has an extensive historical and genealogical collection, as well as archival material which includes includes manuscript collections and more than 2,000 Fullerton negatives. Reproductions of images from the Fullerton Collection may be obtained through the library by contacting the Society, located at 300 West Main Street, Riverhead, NY 11901. The Suffolk County Historical Society is an authorized agency of Suffolk County and is partially funded by the County of Suffolk, Patrick G. Halpin, County Executive. The Society's museum and library are open to the public on a regular basis. For further information, including current hours, call the Suffolk County Historical Society at (516) 727–2881.

The Suffolk County Historical Society, Riverhead.

The Long Island Studies Institute

The Long Island Studies Institute at Hofstra University encourages the study of Long Island's history and heritage through its publications, conferences, educational services, and reference collections. The Institute was established in 1985, when the Nassau County Museum Reference Library moved from the Museum in Eisenhower Park to Hofstra to join the University's New York State History Collections as part of the Department of Special Collections, in the Axinn Library. The Institute also houses the historical research offices of the Nassau County Historian and Division of Museum Services. For information on Institute conferences, publications, and collections (including hours open to the public), contact the Long Island Studies Institute, Axinn Library, Hofstra University, Hempstead, NY 11550; 516–463–5092.

Axinn Library, Hofstra University.